PENGU

THE PENGUIN METAPHYSICAL LIBRARY
General Editor: Jacob Needleman

TO LIVE WITHIN

Lizelle Reymond was born in the early part of this century in Neuchâtel, Switzerland. As a child, she traveled widely with her parents and enjoyed an extensive private education in art, music, and literature. When she was twenty, she became a librarian at the League of Nations, a post she held until World War II. After the war, she left Europe for Calcutta to begin the long series of Indian experiences that have inspired so much of her writing, including *My Life with a Brahmin Family* and the present volume. Madame Reymond now lives in Geneva.

Lizelle Reymond

TO LIVE WITHIN

Foreword by Jacob Needleman

*Translated from the French
by Nancy Pearson
and Stanley Spiegelberg*

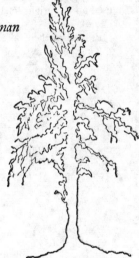

Penguin Books Inc *Baltimore · Maryland*

Penguin Books Inc
7110 Ambassador Road
Baltimore, Maryland 21207, U.S.A.

La Vie dans la vie first published by Editions du Mont-Blanc,
Geneva 1969
First published in English by Doubleday & Company, Inc. 1971
Published in Penguin Books 1973

Printed in the United States of America by
Kingsport Press, Inc., Kingsport, Tennessee

THE PENGUIN METAPHYSICAL LIBRARY

The Penguin Metaphysical Library offers books that can recall in modern man the forgotten knowledge of how to search for himself, knowledge he has lost in his haste to make himself comfortable in the world. From the most diverse geographical origins and historical periods, and from a wide variety of traditions and literary forms, the editor has selected for this series books that have the common goal of orienting man in the search for consciousness.

Throughout the Western world, the realization is dawning that contemporary science, including psychology, provides nothing for man that can take the place of the struggle for self-knowledge, and that most of our present religions have cut themselves off from the energy in their original teachings. Thus a great many Westerners are now seeking out ancient and modern texts that consider human life within cosmic schemes more purposeful than the universe of modern science.

But the understanding of how to relate these writings to our own lives remains elusive. Even the most serious and best informed among us are not sure which ideas are important and which are unnecessary for a real inner search to begin. Therefore, out of this flood of esoteric, traditional, and mystical writings, the editor has chosen only material that bears on the aim of looking impartially and with fresh hope at the chaos we see within ourselves and in the world around us.

JACOB NEEDLEMAN

ACKNOWLEDGMENT

I feel sincere gratitude to the Marsden Foundation for faithful assistance in the years of preparing and writing this book. And to Nancy Pearson I wish to give special thanks for her major contribution in the English translation.

Lizelle Reymond

America is now experiencing a surge of interest in the religious teachings of the East, and thousands of our young people are turning to them. In our need to break through the clichés that have long surrounded these teachings we have not been helped very much by the many new translations of Eastern sacred writings that have so abruptly become available, nor by the dozens of comparative religious studies that have also appeared in recent years. We still suffer from the feeling that the Eastern way is to escape from reality.

To Live Within is both a tale of one Westerner's psychological pilgrimage and a glimpse into the mind of her Master, Shrî Anirvân. Being both of these together, it can serve to deepen our questions about the nature of spiritual work—not only in the traditions of India, but in the heart of all life.

In *My Life With a Brahmin Family*, Lizelle Reymond described how her stay in India became concentrated into the personal discovery that there are laws to spiritual growth quite as exact as anything science has discovered in external nature. Living as part of a traditional family in which all personal life was a search for an active sensitivity to these laws, she wrote of how she finally tasted the true wellspring of Indian spiritual intelligence—in the midst of life, and not apart from it.

Uniquely demanding as this experience was for a Western woman, it was but a preparation for her life with the Master whose teaching is the subject of this book. Here, in the deceptively straightforward narrative of Part I, we are given an inkling of the constant inner price she was willing to pay for the grains of real self-knowledge that the Master made possible amid the demands of setting up a house devoted to sacred work.

Searching for the sense of the *discipline* in this process of sacred work, the reader may notice that Shrî Anirvân never imposes suffering on his pupil. His essential silence helps her, rather, to bear the study both of her automatic suffering and her automatic satisfactions, and therefore to see her life for what it really is.

Serious students of our own Western traditions may take this as a sign that the gap which separates Christianity from Hinduism is not as great as it appears in the familiar formulations. Near to the core of each is the sense of a life task: to learn from a teacher how to work from within with an alertness born of patience and need. When, for example, Lizelle Reymond first writes to Shrî Anirvân inquiring after some texts, she recognizes in his response that although her request was denied, *she* was not. This discrimination comes from need.

We may assume that there is in every man the same exuberant desire for commitment that is written so large in the massive Eastward turn of modern youth. This exuberance almost defines what is most hopeful in American society. But, recognizing this in ourselves, we shall be better prepared for the hard work of understanding the main portions of this book, which demands of us something far more organic than an intellect in the service of exuberance. Perhaps the sacred writings of all times—Christian, Hebrew, Islamic, Buddhist, and Hindu—have spoken to this undiscovered place in us where the lust for commitment is dwarfed by the wish for being.

We must therefore be prepared for mere passing glimpses of the exactitude of Part II. Here the Master speaks in his own words of the path, of consciousness, of awakening, and of life-in-death, ideas that can magnetize the heart of man, but that are almost always crucified by the swift compromises of our outward-directed minds.

Never before has this teaching appeared in the West. If it is a source teaching, that is, a system of ideas that of themselves have the energy to penetrate through the self-deceptions of intellect and ordinary feeling, we may well suspect that it is not enough simply to read this book and to be touched by it. Perhaps that would be our mistake. Can we accept that there exist ideas that have the power to awaken? That these ideas, coming through the medium of a great Master, demand of us only that we not remain closed to them? Then, what is the nature of our effort? What in man resists true ideas? Perhaps the first sense of sacred work, lifelong and arduous, is the effort to study the obstacles in us to an inner divinity that can be neither conquered nor assumed.

Jacob Needleman
Department of Philosophy
San Francisco State College

CONTENTS

CONTENTS

TO LIVE WITHIN

PART I

LIFE IN A HIMALAYAN HERMITAGE

Lizelle Reymond

I.

Introduction

A few months ago I reopened the notebooks filled day by day during the years I lived in the Himalayas. These notes tell the story, as a Hindu would put it, of how I served a Master and of how I came under a spiritual discipline based on the *Sâmkhya* teaching.

I did not publish them sooner because I was obeying a rule that was often stated in my presence. It applied to me just as much as to the others who were following the same teaching:

"Let twelve years go by before speaking about your life here, before forming an evaluation on any subject whatsoever. What will have ripened in you, what will have taken root in your life on all levels will belong to you. Nothing else. Everything you hear has been said thousands of times over thousands of years, and in many different ways. But who is there to listen to it, to understand it, to live it? The living spirituality of India is made up of the sum of the experiences of those who have walked the way before us. In the name of what would you harvest the fruit of another's sacrifice before having paid the price yourself?"

I asked the Master, "May I mention your name?" He thought awhile and then answered, "Yes, if you like, but I hope you will use it very simply, like a peg on which very ancient thoughts have been hung that are not of my making, nor of yours. But don't be in a hurry to write about all this. Remember that our understanding of life progresses at the speed of a bullock cart. The impatient man runs, greedy for conquest. Our mind has wings and can soar over difficulties, but we have a fine pair of feet to keep in touch with Mother Earth. We have to plow through it and often stumble over roots and stones. Then comes the time for sowing. Our feet dance in joy and this spontaneous joy is the daughter of our soul. Remember that all the real things in life are in accord with a very slow rhythm like the changing of seasons and the coursing of stars. This work in depth is done in darkness, without sound."

Seated around Shrî Anirvân on one day or another were Hindus, Buddhists, Christians, Muslims—believers or unbelievers—each one carried by his own discipline, his own effort, his own ideal; each one receiving the food he was in need of. We were learning, day after day, how to live within.

II

Meeting with Myself

I first heard of Shrî Anirvân when I was living at Nârâyan Tewari Dewal, near Almora. I was working on the translation of a book. When I had finished my task, I began to look for sacred texts to send to my publisher. A wandering *sâdhu* —little knowing the role he was to play in my life—told me about Shrî Anirvân, an independent monk, very learned, who lived in a distant village, and who was translating the *Third Mandala of the Vedas* into Bengali. This monk received no one.

I decided to write to him to ask for Vedic texts to be published in France. I doubted whether he would answer. However, a month later a reply came: a refusal. But one sentence in the letter attracted my attention. I decided to write again. This time, without mentioning texts for translation, I spoke from myself asking a question about spiritual discipline.

Two weeks passed. A letter arrived that, with the directness that had already impressed me, gave a date for an appointment two months later after the rainy season. Shrî Anirvân lived in a valley at right angles to the one where I was living, some sixty miles from Almora. In order to get there across the hill-tops, I would have to hire a guide and a porter and count on a four-day march. I answered, accepting the appointment suggested and undertaking to arrive on the day and at the hour stated.

I have a rather confused memory of the three days I spent in Shrî Anirvân's Lohaghat hermitage as I was neither prepared for the welcome I was given nor capable of understanding it. The travel notes from that year show that my only preoccupation was to miss nothing of what was said in front of me, to take in everything that happened and engrave it on my memory so as to be able later to recapture the same current of thought.

Nothing was as I had expected. Shrî Anirvân was neither a Master of *yoga*, nor of spiritual discipline, nor of traditional philosophy; as a result, having spent years in India searching for just these various paths of knowledge, I felt suddenly at a loss. I was consciously aware of a feeling that everything to which I had been most attached was fading away. In Shrî Anirvân's room no altar was to be seen, no pictures of the gods, just a vista of blue mountains through the french windows.

Shrî Anirvân appeared frail. He was shy. He wore a long white robe and had a black beard. He had interrupted his work to receive me and had prepared the tea himself. A local cloth merchant who had done some traveling had advised him to serve it to me in a porcelain cup, which had been brought for the purpose. His eyes laughed at my confusion on being shown so much attention, and also with his own pleasure in being able to offer me freshly cracked nuts. He explained that a friend had brought food prepared especially for me and that the same thing would be done the next day. I gathered that he lived on offerings and that everyone around him knew about my visit.

Although I scarcely remember the words that were exchanged, I retain, nevertheless, a deep impression of the hours of silence passed on the terrace of his house where, seated before him, I found myself for the first time "alone in front of myself." There was nothing left of the emotional impulses that I had known in some spiritual disciplines—impulses of devotion, of self-abandonment, of submission, of a sudden understanding of what was beyond me, of gratitude to those on my path who had opened my heart and mind; this time I felt alone and laid bare in my own inner life. And his look held me to the awareness of the moment without any possibility of escape.

On the third day I left without knowing whether we would ever see each other again. I went to Calcutta. There, during the winter, Shrî Anirvân came to see me.

I was at a crossroads in my personal life, in a strange kind of freedom that had cost much suffering. I was facing a choice. But to know the direction rested entirely on one question: "What is my place in the universe?" I no longer know whether I said those words aloud, but he answered them: "There I think I can be useful to you, but the road is stony. . . ."

On hearing these words, I came to an immediate decision: to work with Shrî Anirvân, if he would allow me that privilege, under any conditions whatsoever and no matter where. He suggested that I should come to him at the hermitage that I already knew, but not until six months later. Nothing was said about the "gap in time" that was to pass between the moment of my decision and the time of my departure for the Himalayas—a period during which, as it happened, all the opposing currents were unleashed to hinder me from following my way.

Shrî Anirvân asked me to bring some kerosene, a lamp with two spare globes, and a minimum of personal things. Apart from that, for as long as he would keep me with him, I was to live, according to tradition, entirely under the discipline of his School, on what he would give me, and without being allowed on my side to give anything at all. I was to receive everything from him: food for my body, his teaching and the instruction necessary to enable me to assimilate it on my level of understanding. I was going to discover an aim in every hour of the day, to live my own life as a direct experience, however humble, at the heart of life. In Shrî Anirvân, I had chosen a Master whose gentleness was equaled only by his firmness.

By letter he established our future relationship: "I shall be free for you twice a day, the first time after five o'clock, before one of my friends arrives—when he is here, he sits down without disturbing me, sometimes asks a question, and meditates. The second time will be after the evening meal. I know there will be many questions we shall have to discuss together, but if we do it regularly and methodically, we shall say a lot in one hour. The rest of the time, night and day, the house will be plunged in the silence of the Void, so that you will not be able even to feel that somebody is living there beside you."

Having protected himself in this way from invasion, he failed to add that his kindness and comprehension would follow me step by step. I had a room facing west, with eucalyptus trees, yuccas and ferns outside my french window—a table and a chair in addition to the writing board placed on the floor in the customary way. Some fruit, some sweetmeats were sent to me whenever he received any. And between one conversation and the next my solitude was filled by my vigilant effort to discover myself. I guessed that I was being put to the test. And the test lasted several months without respite.

A young servant used to come for two hours every day, bringing water and milk and to peel and cut up vegetables. I used to make myself a cup of tea early in the morning. The happy surprise for me was the chief meal of the day at eleven o'clock, which Shrî Anirvân himself prepared. We ate sitting on the floor, side by side, absorbed in the thought of our work. Occasionally, he would speak to me very openly, helping me to catch the trend of his thinking. When this happened, the hours that followed would be filled with cheerful pictures!

In the afternoon I used to take a walk alone in the forest, rather fearfully at first, for as soon as dusk fell one would hear the call of wild beasts. This long period of solitude taught me to be very simple in my movements, my attitudes, my words; to find what was essential in my relationship with Shrî Anirvân—a deep accord.

Then came the monsoon. Enormous black clouds climbed up the mountains and burst with a crash; the whole of nature was impregnated with mist and it penetrated into the rooms. The high grass was covered with leeches. I no longer went out. This was a time meant for study, for retreat.

The walls of my room and those of Shrî Anirvân's room were lined with books—a library classified by subjects, some four thousand volumes on the esoterics of Eastern traditions. I had taken down a few books from the shelves, haphazardly, in order to escape from my own thoughts rather than to study. Shrî Anirvân made no comment. Without interfering, he watched me live.

In the obscurity of my search, when I came to realize that there was only *myself* setting out to discover *I am*, something became disjointed. Did I accept being helpless and being aware of it? I had become afraid, with an instinctive fear of losing something precious, whereas the right move would have been to hold onto the slender thread which I guessed was the link between *me* and *I am*. If I was able for a few seconds to experience this as a certainty, the pursuit came to a stop, only to start up again very soon and with greater intensity. Then Shrî Anirvân came forth with a suggestion: "Try to see that relaxation is nothing but the transformation of something rigid into something supple, if to it you add a notion of expansion."

I tried it, as hour after hour I attempted to follow the path of my thought. The very question, "Who am I?" had a snare in it that I tried to avoid. There was the risk that I would become attached to the question like a miser to his gold and lose sight of my real aim in a new kind of slavery. This aim was a light shining through the fog. I sensed its warmth in me, which was all I could perceive of the consciousness towards which I was groping my way.

I had arrived at the Lohaghat hermitage defeated by life, having given up everything I had believed to be a possible answer, according to Hinduism, to the "Why?" of life. Hindu philosophy, I knew, was divided into watertight compartments, learnedly expounded by intelligent monks in order to capture the attention of the West: *yogas* of asceticism, of knowledge, of action, of love, which in India formed a solid whole. Rites owing allegiance to many faiths and a wide variety of customs flowed out from these in a materiality enfolding all possible concepts of life. By then I had given up looking into all these philosophical teachings and instead had plunged into everyday life as it is lived amongst the people of the cities and villages, among the refugees who, at that time, were pouring in from Pakistan stripped of all their possessions. This had brought me to understand why the vision of the Lord Krishna dancing to the sound of his flute enchants the Hindu in his poverty and why we of the West, enjoying a profusion of everything, worship the Man-God dying on His Cross.

Shrî Anirvân smiled at my outbursts. In a practical way I had discovered why any discipline, whatever it may be, can be pictured as a wheel whose rim exerts constant pressure inwards, in the direction of the hub, where the *Ishtadevatâ*, or chosen image of the Divine, stands, but I did not yet know that to be attached to an *Ishtadevatâ* is just as precarious as to be attached to some human love. Adolescent love stands up neither to the pressure of facts nor to the hazards of life.

Cracks in my outer shell were opening one after another, each time exposing some new zone of darkness in my understanding. At the moment I am speaking of, all inner feeling being rejected, an extraordinarily dry period ensues, during which the Master's hand is indispensable. Discrimination gives rise to contradictions, in the midst of which one struggles; one lives without love, without patience. The vital attachment one had felt with those around one and the tasks undertaken lose their meaning; the aim, hitherto considered indispensable, becomes blurred. The imaginary ideal is broken. This is a cruel moment, but a necessary one, until there arises from the depths of one's being a new, more contained, though still eager, impulse.

Since every Master sees the influences that govern the pupils who come to him, I had admitted to myself that since Shrî Anirvân was keeping me near him, it meant that a certain inner work was possible under his direction. There was not the least sentimentality in our relationship, but an expression perhaps of deep respect and commitment to a mutual responsibility. Our life was like a harmonic chord with exactly known intervals.

For my part, I knew that if Shrî Anirvân had given me a place, one day, in the same way, he would send me away. With a touch of disguised effrontery, I had asked him, "When will you send me away from here?" He answered seriously, looking at me quietly, "When you have found your place in life, you will have nothing more to do here."

One evening, after the usual meditation hour, Shrî Anirvân told me his plans for leaving Lohaghat. As it happened, our hermitage, hanging as it did on a mountainside, was too precarious a place in which to remain the whole year and to receive the pupils who were asking to come from Bengal and Assam. The road was dangerous in the rainy season. At that time it was really only a track that was washed away and disappeared in some of the river beds. One had to go through a jungle where tigers, leopards, and wild elephants were coming into their own again. Nobody willingly ventured into it. The mails were rare, the postman making the ascent only once a week.

Of course, the monks in the Mayavatî monastery that perched on a hill opposite were only too glad to spend their winters in that isolated retreat created by Swâmi Vivekânanda, but our plans made it necessary to remain in touch with life. It was up to us to find a less trying and more accessible environment.

It was decided that I should go ahead to Almora, which I already knew from having stayed there twice for long periods.[1]

My journey across the mountains was uneventful. The Joshi family was waiting for me. Bepin, a young lawyer, put himself at my disposal for they were all anxious for Shrî Anirvân to come and settle in Almora.

The very next day Bepin took me to look at three houses. The first two were too spacious for us and the rent too high. The third one, four miles outside the town, was built on the edge of the forest. It faced south, and its deserted terraces

[1] *My Life With a Brahmin Family* (London: Rider & Co., 1958; New York: Roy Publishers, 1960).

and solidly constructed outbuildings had disappeared behind the overgrown mimosas.

Forewarned, the owner was waiting for us on the spot. As I went forward to meet this paunchy lawyer who was twirling a silver-knobbed walking stick, he began in a shrill voice to boast about his house as though it had been a palace. In actual fact, every windowpane had been replaced by planks. Moss and cactus were growing between the cracks in the paving. A few worm-eaten pieces were all that represented furniture in the house itself. The roof was leaking. The owner's arrogance and his comical arguments were irritating, but the place was suitable. I decided to take it at all costs. After lengthy discussion, a lease was signed.

I was thrilled and still full of joy when I went that evening to pay a courtesy visit to the late Pandit Joshi's uncle. This austere Brahmin always made me shy, although I knew he liked me. I would need his support in order to be accepted in the closed society of Almora and in my future dealings with the inhabitants of the small village near the new house.

He received me seated on a woven grass mat, the *Bhagavad Gîtâ* open in front of him. In a niche hollowed out in the wall, incense and an oil lamp were burning before the picture of the Lord Krishna, his *Ishtadevatâ*. Uncle Biren knew that since I had neither old parents to care for nor children to bring up, it was incumbent on me freely to find my own direction toward the inner disciplines. From his point of view, logically and clearly, I was entering the third *âshrama* of my life.[2] "But how would you know the Divine if you do not know yourself?" he asked me. "What dwelling place would you be able to offer Him? It takes a long time to prepare the heart for the inflow of the divine Name, like a wave pouring into the hollow of a rock."

Through his nephew, Uncle Biren knew about the work of

---

[2] *Vânaprastha*, the stage of spiritual search.

translating sacred writings of India with which I had been associated in Europe. He knew that I had sat at the feet of Masters who had given me their grace so that I might have access to the "sensitive heart." But the real work was only now beginning, in direct experience, lived under control. He was glad to know that I had decided to stay at Almora as long as might be necessary in order to distill and put into practice what I was receiving.

"On the esoteric level your decision is justified," said Uncle Biren. "One has to taste and to recognize what one receives, and learn to find it again, day after day, for this taste fades easily. Often nothing remains but the memory of it. Just as with a plant, one has to let it grow and develop without fear of apparent frustrations. Then alone does the inner flowering become possible—on our level, it goes without saying. The resistance comes from the hardened covering, but this conceals the kernel of palpitating life. Have confidence; obey without asking questions. In this way the being will come to have priority over the ego. Be blessed in your effort."

On the following day I returned to Lohaghat with the signed lease in my bag. In time with the rhythm of my footsteps, I was already organizing the new house in my thought, putting a nail in here and there, painting the shelves, pulling out an odd bush, planting hollyhock, arranging trellises around the windows. By the time I arrived at the hermitage, our future house in Almora was practically restored!

Shrî Anirvân, as always, was writing on the veranda. He barely raised his head. His look was calm and full of peace. Face to face with him, I suddenly felt how false my inner attitude was and how difficult it is, in words that are simple and right, to give account of an assignment one has carried out. He listened attentively, then said, "Well, I shall live in the little outbuilding at the bottom of the garden from where one can see the river. The men will live in the building on the lower level and you in the big house with the women."

"So you know this house?"

"No, I have only seen it through your eyes," he answered.
"May this house be open to the spirit, to life. For now, let
go of it, the better to hold onto it."

And he began to recite a poem:

> . . . and one day the Bâüls[3]
> came into the house.
> They sang, danced and drank
> and then they went away
> and the house remained empty. . . .

Shrî Anirvân sat still. My arrival had interrupted him in the
middle of the sentence he was writing and now, with his pen
raised, he was waiting for me to go away before continuing.

There was a long pause without any movement. Standing,
ill at ease, I felt the tears running down my cheeks. I put the
lease down in front of him and went away.

This house at Almora had invaded my thought. It was driv-
ing me out of myself, preventing me from working. Shrî
Anirvân did not speak of it, nor did I. How were we ever
going to move all those books, without crates, without ser-
vants, without money? I lived with a deep sense of shame.
Then, in order to tame the rebellious mind, I began to learn a
Sanskrit hymn by heart and recited it in the forest to the
trees and the mountains.

One evening, Shrî Anirvân suggested, "In the future house
it will be good if we study some hymns of praise to the
great forces of nature. They will be chosen from the *Vedas*.
What do you say? Starting tomorrow morning we will begin
to pack the books. Punetha has brought up some canvas for
that purpose."

[3] Wandering mystics, known for their songs, absolutely simple, very
profound.

III

Haïmavatî

We left in December. There was already hoarfrost on the ground and the mountains glistened with fresh snow. A small truck followed us with the books; the rest mattered little.

Shrî Anirvân left immediately for Delhi where his disciples awaited him. Ahead of him were three months of wandering from town to town as far as Bengal and Assam.

My own task was to open the house in Almora and prepare myself for the life that would come to fill it. When we parted, Shrî Anirvân had said, "It is good that you are going to the new house by yourself and will live there quietly, in retreat. Certainly you can absorb new ideas and make them your own, but later you will have to create freely your own way of expressing them. That is the work of the active power [*Shakti*]. And it can only be done in silence. I can help you to find your own power, suggest a way, a means, for you to approach it, but nothing more. I never impose anything; I love freedom too much, and so do you! I am not expecting anything in particular and have no preconceived or stereotyped idea about you. I shall only be glad if you open your petals and you, yourself, find yourself."

I arrived at Almora the next day, late in the afternoon, and was happy to find Bepin Joshi at the entrance to the town. He was there to warn me that the road up the hill was blocked by a landslide. The bales of books had been unloaded by the roadside. I was somewhat alarmed when I saw a horde of Nepalese coolies rushing at me and asking to be hired as porters. Bepin finally chose about fifteen men, as well as some torchbearers for the trip through the forest. What a procession! Bent double under the heavy bales of books hanging in leather straps, the men kept shouting at each other—a violent rhythm that punctuated the march.

I was exhausted by their efforts, ashamed because of their sweat, their fatigue, their tatters, their gaunt legs—all this so that our "knowledge" should shortly be arranged on the shelves that the carpenter had just finished. And I was imagining in advance the uproar there would be when the men scrambled for their shares of the few rupees that I was going to give them.

That first night I made acquaintance with the forest, the wind rustling in the pines, the yapping of the jackals together with the furious barking of the dogs, and then, early in the morning, the notes of a skillfully played pipe, repeated over and over like a prayer.

Shrî Anirvân had suggested that this house on a hill in the forest be called "Haïmavatî." In the *Kena Upanishad*[1] Haïmavatî is the immaterial whiteness, the daughter of the sky who incarnates the principle of expansion on the terrestrial plane. As snow she falls lightly, piles up, is transformed into ice so

[1] 3.12.

that torrents may flow from its energy. In silence, she is a blessing from the sky to the earth.

The hill stretches to the rock of Kasardevî, a natural hollow, like a matrix of the world, where human sacrifices were undoubtedly offered up in the old days. A vast landscape extends to the horizon—valleys and mountain ranges, on the summits of which dwell goddesses in tiny white temples. Almora, however full of light, nevertheless remains a land of dissolution (*pralaya*), its beauty lying in the bareness of its mountainsides and the play of light on stone.

Below the house the road winds from terrace to terrace down to the bank of the River Koshî where the dead are burned. The green of rice or wheat alternates, according to the season, with the russet shade of the earth.

From a distance Shrî Anirvân followed what I was doing; I kept him informed. A month after my arrival he wrote me:

"I am so glad to learn that the toil and moil of putting the house in order is over, and that you have settled down again to your personal work in a quiet rhythm. I know you will not mind if my letter is short since I have nothing to say. Only one thing is important; become an adult! You are responsible for the first atmosphere of Haïmavatî. May this house resound with the call of the Vedic sages: 'Live, and move about in the atmosphere of the Vast!'[2] Let all our friends come soon, may they hasten to visit Haïmavatî. For her alone, the force which is the child of the Void! Let no one come for you or for me! Let everybody throw off all poses, all trammels, and stand nude in the silence ready to bathe in its light until his soul is drenched by it. Discover yourself, identify yourself with the profound dumb power of the earth which silently fashions the dark clay into a spray of sun-kissed blossoms. You have this power in you, but you do not yet know it.

---

[2] *"Vasa brahmacaryam"* (*Chhândogya Up.* 6.1.1.)

It is the power of the dark night holding its breath in order to give birth to the new dawn."

A few days later he wrote again:

"I could not bear Haïmavatî to become a rendezvous. It must be a deep pool of life wherein one must plunge to live in death. And the *work*. This work is not a pretext to be taken lightly. It is a deep inner work in the rhythm of the heart of life. It is creation. For the moment, you can do but one thing—create in yourself respect for your own work, for your own effort, in silence, and with the discipline you are approaching."

I was impatient, and at the same time I had an unacknowledged fear of what was going to take place. I came and went in the empty whitewashed rooms of the house, which were waiting for life to fill them. Rope beds had been made on the spot as well as stools and a low table for the refectory.

Speaking of his pupils, Shrî Anirvân wrote:

"A great period of interiorization has taken hold of them. I have planted a seed in their hearts and done my part of the work. I have only to wait, but without desire, without expectation. I may see a mighty oak grow or the seed may rot . . . My days are so full that I cannot snatch even half an hour to write letters. So I give up! The people who come to see me are so kind, so quiet and so free. They are cultivating their soil. I give them all my time. About your own work, do not force yourself. There is no hurry about anything. Remember the Bàül's song:

> O stubborn one, by your cruel impatience,
> by your merciless insistence,
> by the fire do you really wish
> to force tight buds to open, flowers to bloom
> and fill the air with their perfume?

So, let Haïmavatî grow and let these things find their own place while calmly observing their movement. To be a tangent that touches the circle of energy at one point only without twining oneself round it—that is the whole secret of life!"

Shrî Anirvân arrived a few days before his pupils. News travels quickly in India among the élite. The idea of establishing a Cultural Center where Hinduism and Islam would be studied side by side, where seekers would be received who would dedicate a part or the whole of their lives to collecting and translating texts hitherto unknown and having them published by Indian universities, resulted in an offer from patrons in Delhi, Allahabad, and the South to follow our work and bring us substantial help. The first to arrive was a Muslim from the South who was translating texts from the *Upanishads* into arabic.

Shrî Anirvân's dream was taking shape, or so I was only too ready to imagine, since my enthusiasm created conditions favorable to this train of thought. In addition to my personal work, I felt myself free to carry a big share of the responsibility for the practical organization of our Cultural Center. Shrî Anirvân was much more cautious, knowing how, in India, although the mind may be free and discussion open, custom shackles and crushes those who do not obey the caste laws.

Three Hindu pupils arrived together, two women and a man. I welcomed them from the top of the terrace steps with open arms; they greeted me with respect. Our entire relationship had to be built from nothing since everything separated us except the idea of serving the same aim—language, manners, food, all sorts of habits associated since childhood with attitudes toward the sacred.

Of course I had set up a plan for running the house and Shrî Anirvân had watched me doing it. Bepin had chosen a high-caste servant for me so that everyone should feel at ease, and indeed everyone was except I, for I could no longer go into the kitchen! A Buddhist writer who arrived at this point used to eat in his room, coming to join us only for the study groups. I understood that the more I effaced myself, the less I would disturb everybody's movements. Seeing my embarrassment, Shrî Anirvân had remarked, "In this house you will be the eye which sees nothing. One can inspire another by one's way of living, allowing each one the freedom to search for himself and set up his own way of life."

One morning, one of the two women, a widow, came to see me. She was small, unusually energetic. She was a barrister in a big eastern city and spoke English fluently. She brought me a poem to translate from the Hindi. She sat on the floor and began to recite the verses, clapping the rhythm with her hands. Then by an ingenious word-for-word process, we passed into English and then into French. While the words slipped from one to the other, something else came to life between us and made it possible for us to share the same experience. In the evening, during the study hour, we sat side by side, each with one hand open and stretched out toward the other to make sure of the other's approval. Nandinî called me "Mother" because I was the older. Years later, with the same heartfelt tenderness, she brought her married children to me so that I should know them.

Living so completely removed from any accustomed mode of thinking made my meetings with Shrî Anirvân stand out in an extraordinary way; he saw what a struggle I was having with myself. The wish to concentrate every observation into very short sentences, to put an end intentionally to the outward expression of the inner nature in revolt, necessitated intense work on oneself in which the least reaction became the size of a mountain. In my immediate surroundings I had the same impression of being stranded. Had I not been living in the house of a *sâdhu*, I would certainly have incurred the suspicion of the people of the neighboring village. The fact that I was not English intrigued them. They showed me great respect.

When Shrî Anirvân passed by, the village people called him "Mahâraj" (Lord). In the close circle of his pupils we called him, "*Rishida.*" *Dâ* is an abbreviation for *Dadâ,* which means "elder brother." Shrî Anirvân like this form of address, which created amongst us a certain intimacy and brotherhood. The word "*Rishi,*" of course, calls up the picture of a very old sage absorbed in the study of the revealed writings. While a monk is expected to live in retirement from the world, a *Rishi* has a more independent life; with a *Rishi* at the center of a hermitage, pupils and whole families come to live around him. The *Upanishads* were born from such communities, from their austere search for pure thought. Shrî Anirvân wrote unceasingly. Several philosophical treatises, published in India by institutes for traditional studies, bear his name. At the time when he was living in his Guru's *âshram* his writings were anonymous. Only writings for laymen circulating from hand to hand are signed with his pseudonym, "Satyakâma."

In fact, no one knew very much about his life or about the sources of his teaching, which was so direct and practical. Everyone had his own opinion about this and thought he knew better than the other. It was often the subject between us when we were reading newspapers and letters after meals. If someone asked Shrî Anirvân a question about his life, he would answer precisely, giving atmosphere and background as a framework for the events he was relating; but if he felt the question came from the wish to establish a chronology of his pilgrimages and the periods he had spent in various *âshrams* or brotherhoods, immediately places and dates were intentionally mixed up. Long periods of his life remained unknown. For him, time was of no account except in the relation that exists between the inner life and life in the world. And years lived in a one-pointed search had taught him the art of silence in which time loses its importance. Fifteen years later he himself told me of the first part of his life, perhaps so that I should understand that he had paid a high price for his luminous freedom.

IV

A Bâül

Shrî Anirvân was born in a little town in the east of Bengal like all the other towns in the region: houses with thatched roofs jutting out over circular verandas, beaten earth steps, brass utensils drying in the sun. Everywhere on the outskirts are banana and palm trees and hedges of flowering creepers dividing one garden from the next.

This exuberance flows down to the many ponds covered with lotuses and reeds. Beyond these, the rice fields and pastures stretch to the horizon. Many birds abide there—among them kingfishers and white cranes. Over it all is the sun which burns up everything or the rains which turn the earth to mud. It is all excessive, violent, and at the same time full of tenderness, for the sun's rays play with the dust and with the evening mist.

His father was a doctor. At the age of eleven, like all the

little boys of his caste, he said the ritual prayers in the morning. Every day he recited a chapter of the *Bhagavad Gîtâ*, and on some days Pânini's treatise,[1] scanning the rhythm and marking the long syllables. At school he was a good pupil, anxious to learn because this is why one goes to school and because it is a privilege. One day the teacher who was taking the class, in commenting on a poem, said, "Everything we see is unreal. This is the basis of *Vedanta*."[2]

With the rest of the class, the child repeated the lesson word for word, but when it came to saying: "All that we see is unreal," he was looking at a rosebud that was opening on a bush close to where the pupils were sitting. He saw the birth of his independent thought. "If I am seeing this rose blossoming in front of me, how can I say that it does not exist? Am I seeing this rose? Do I exist? Do I see this rose?" In recitation the next day, he found it impossible to repeat the theme. While hearing it chanted in chorus by the pupils, he was saying to himself: "I, I am alone . . . I don't think like the others. What is going to happen to me? It hurts . . ."

This became a burning question: "When I look at something, does that thing exist?" He felt that behind the question there was no answer. One cannot argue with the schoolmaster any more than with one's father. He felt insolent in his thought and in his heart, and yet his question was alive. Who was going to be able to answer him? He wondered to himself, "And so all I see around me does not exist? But *no*, it is not true!"

From that time on, a secret life took root in him, based on a nagging doubt. Everything around him seemed mechanical, having nothing to do with his living question. The rites and customs methodically determining what was to be done at

[1] A classical grammar book of the fifth century B.C.
[2] One of the six classical schools (*darshanas*) of Hindu philosophy, founded by Bâdarâyâna or Vyâsa and the one that is best known in the West.

every hour of the day lost their content. Yet all the members of the family—brother, sister, mother, grandmother, even his father—conformed to them. Why? He himself continued to submit, out of obedience, to all these requirements, but what was the sense, he wondered, "if nothing exists," of all these rules of life? He looked around him as for the first time, observing what went on, noticing what each person did. Twenty years later, he still remembered things said by every member of his family. Everything seemed to him to be an unreal play without beginning or end.

Several of his father's friends were Muslims. He took refuge with them because they spoke another language. One of them, the head of a large family, was a Sufi. Hindus from the neighborhood liked to visit him because they considered him a pure diamond, full of a caustic wisdom that made them laugh heartily. Sometimes one would hear him wildly lamenting: "Ah, divine freedom, true gift of God, where are you? What are you doing to me? Just look at me, here among my own"—and he would point to his wife, his children, his grandchildren—"I am bothered with so many little worries. If I did not undergo them, I would not know that you exist. So where are you hiding? Why do you not come to me?" And he would begin to sing, making big gestures, his hands opened towards heaven, sometimes weeping, and those who heard him would beat time to the rhythm of his chant. The schoolboy listened eagerly. Where was this divine freedom known to the Sufi? Was it real or unreal? But the child was afraid of a rebuff and did not ask questions. He thought, "I shall find it by myself, I shall go off and search for it."

He began to go to the bank of the Brahmaputra very early in the morning, where Hindus and Muslims used to bathe. He would thread his way between them and pass unnoticed—just one more youngster among those who were shouting and playing around. He used to make his way cautiously towards a pandit who was highly respected by the people around him for his saintly life as well as for his free thinking. The pandit was accustomed to meet on the bank with a Sufi from a neighboring village. After greeting each other, the two men used to chant, each in his own fashion, the one hundred and eight or the ninety-nine Divine Names. Then, while the Sufi repeated tirelessly "*La illâhâ illa Allâ*," the Brahmin, up to the waist in water, proceeded with the rites of his purification, loudly invoking the mystical fire of heaven: "*Marudbhir agna â gahi.*" As soon as he came out of the water, the Sufi stopped praying. Before taking leave of one another, they embraced warmly at length, not caring for the taboos that should have divided them. Some days they would sit down on the stones and, while the bathers made a circle around them, they would tell stories, each in turn. Could the orthodox of the Shariyat and the Brahmin priests from the temple prevent these accolades and the freedom of expression of these two men?

One day, coming out of school, the Hindu boy went with a Muslim schoolfellow down to the riverbank to play. They had a great time jumping into puddles and playing ducks and drakes with carefully selected stones! The sun was high and after a while, worn out, the two youngsters threw themselves on the ground in the shade of a bush. They were hungry. The young Muslim said, "I have something to eat with me; come on, let's share it!" He took a little parcel wrapped in a banana leaf out of his bag, opened it, and held out half of it to his companion. The children began to eat while teasing the tadpoles with their toes.

All of a sudden, the Muslim boy said slyly, "Do you know you have lost caste by eating forbidden things with me? I will tell and everybody will speak of you!" "No, you are wrong," replied his Hindu comrade, surprised. "I am free like Kikirchand.[3] I can eat anything I like, for I am a Bâül and

---

[3] A Hindu Bâül assuming a Muslim name "Kikirchand Fakir" whose songs were very popular then.

I am above all castes." As he spoke, he stood up, for when one says a thing like that, one calls on the sun as a witness. The freedom that was ripening in him burst out. "I am a Bâul seeking for divine freedom and nothing will hold me back." But at the same time it was clear to him that he would have to submit to the classical traditional disciplines—no matter which —if he wished to go towards the freedom he longed for and towards the expansion of the self. He had already understood that one can only grow starting from the seed that one is and that a sure road is a necessity. At that very instant, he knew that his search had begun.

Carried away by the idea of becoming a *sâdhu* in quest of the supreme freedom, he found that nothing else counted any more. He meekly accepted all rules, all fasts, telling himself that they were milestones on the road. He began to read all he could find about the lives of saints and masters.

Now at this time his father, who was very devout, came by chance on a book of instruction in *yoga* that contained a portrait of the author. Fascinated by the expression of his face, he decided to find this man and invite him to his house. He wrote his intention to his son, who was spending a few weeks' holiday with an uncle in the north of the province.

When the boy received the letter, it was a shock. He left immediately, and in order to get home quickly, he walked even during the hottest hours of the day, repeating over and over like a prayer: "I am on the way to meet my *Thakur,*[4] a man who has reached the goal! He is my *Thakur!*" But on reaching home, he was disappointed to learn that the monk would not arrive for another three months. He waited for him with the same song of enthusiasm in his heart. His ideal created in advance the food of which he was in need. He was tormented by the idea of God. One night, the vision of a long road

[4] Lord, the Divine incarnate. A name given by every disciple to his Guru.

reaching to the horizon, and of himself making his way on it, reassured him as to his destiny.

When the monk finally appeared,[5] the boy knew as soon as he saw him that he was not mistaken—he was the man to guide him, to lead him to reach the three stages of consciousness spoken of in the Scriptures—*Sat-Chit-Ânanda*.[6] The Swâmi had something majestic about him, something as wide as the sky. In the very moment of giving himself up to the Master, however, the boy knew in the depths of his being that he already possessed the freedom he wanted to find. It had been revealed to him one night when he was barely nine years old. That night the sky with all its stars had entered into him, throwing him to the ground in a swoon. He had never spoken of it because there were no right words to describe it, but the secret bloomed in him like a lotus when he heard Kikirchand sing; it filled his heart and tears ran down his cheeks.

He gave himself passionately to this man Guru who was absolutely necessary to him, holding nothing back, repeating to himself: "I love him, I am going to serve him, to follow him, for he is my *Thakur*." The Swâmi was thirty-eight years old. Elegantly dressed, his hair falling in curls to his shoulders, a ring on his right hand, he gave the impression of belonging to the world rather than to a monastic order. He had learned from several teachers the practical disciplines that gave directives for life. Open, natural, with great yogic powers, this man embodied a mystery.

For three years, the Swâmi's visits were repeated at regular intervals. In between, the father of the family used to go to visit him, each time coming back transformed, full of stories of spiritual disciplines and ecstatic states which he told to his

[5] Swâmi Nigamânanda (Joy of Vedic realization), died 1935. His place of burial is in Halisahar, Bengal.
[6] Pure Existence, Pure Spirit, Pure Bliss.

wife. His young son listened with a growing hunger for a life like that for himself.

The Swâmi was planning to settle in Assam, where the government was giving away land to anyone prepared to drain it. This was virgin territory, swampy and malarial. A first group of disciples was ready to accompany the Swâmi and dedicate themselves to the service of their fellow man while living in accordance with the law of the *Shastras*. To struggle against untamed nature, virgin forests, and wild beasts seemed to go hand in hand with the conquest of the inner nature.

A decisive moment arrived. One night the father woke up his son in order to have a talk with him. "Listen. In a year you will be sixteen; you will be a man. You will become the head of the family, for I have decided to go with your mother to live at the feet of the Guru in Assam. Your grandmother will take care of the younger children. Money has been set aside for your studies. You will become a doctor like me."

The boy, who had never spoken openly with his father, felt the earth giving way under his feet. Out of respect he was bound to obey and he said not a word. How could he have cried out, "I, too. I want to go to him—he is my *Thakur!* All I long for is the life described in the *Upanishads,* to serve the Guru and to reach the goal!"

He remained silent and for seven months struggled with himself. At last, one night, he pulled the bolts, went out, closed the door behind him, padlocked it, and went away without taking a leave of anyone. He visualized his *Thakur* in a halo of freedom, but when he arrived there, nothing he had expected was given him—no teaching, no discipline. Life in the *âshram*-to-be was a medley of the sounds of hammers, saws, and picks. It was centered entirely on unconditional love for the Guru and self-effacement. The one call was to action: "Work for the Guru!" which meant digging wells and ditches, cutting down trees, building houses. In his devotion, the young man accepted all the circumstances as they were. He worked without thinking, to the limit of his strength. Sweat and tears together streamed down his face. He did not notice them.

After a few months, news came that he had been awarded a State Scholarship on the results of the University examination he had sat for before he left. The Guru made the decision: "Well! If that is so, then you go and study! I shall need a well-educated man like you later on."

And so the young man went away for six whole years, first to Dacca, then to the University of Calcutta. He worked hard, dreaming of his Guru. When he came back to the *âshram* for vacations, the Master made him welcome, kept him constantly at his side, and told him in detail about everything that was going on. The disciples considered him the great favorite—the poet who sang his devotion and was able to open all hearts. He was liked because what he said drove out fatigue and transported the mind above the realm of the senses. He served the Guru in all things, fanning him during the oppressive nights, attending upon him in little details. Love of the Guru filled his life.

After passing his examinations brilliantly, the student was getting ready to return to the *âshram* for good. On his last day in Calcutta something occurred that left its mark on his life and changed its course. On the way to the station where he was to take the train for Assam, he looked around him as for the first time and, relaxed, smiled at the people, amused by everything he was seeing, absorbing the life around him.

A fog came down. He shook himself as though he were coming out of a long sleep, his limbs numb. Where was he? He shut his eyes. In a vision, he saw the gentle banks of the Brahmaputra, the vast sky, himself standing between earth and heaven in his own freedom. He heard the murmur of the water running over the pebbles. Who was he? A wandering Bâül? He was seized by an irresistible impulse to go towards the South, all the way to Cape Comorin, to see the goddess Kanya Kumarî[7] with his own eyes, in her eternal waiting, the infinity of the seas, the infinity of freedom.

He decided at once that he would take a ticket to Kanya Kumarî and that he would not return to the *âshram*. He arrived at the station and took his place in the line of travelers waiting to buy tickets. For a long while there in the crowd he knew the joy of being in harmony with himself. But when he came to the ticket office window he found it impossible to utter a single word. He felt pushed from behind, jostled. Then he distinctly heard a voice saying: "One third-class ticket to Jorhat in Assam." He shut his eyes and knew that he had just been swallowed by his Guru.

When he arrived at the *âshram*, a complete change in his way of life was awaiting him. Books were put aside. He took his place as a novice beside the other monks, the diggers, the plowmen, the woodcutters. The life was hard. The Guru imposed silence during the work. The clearing of the undergrowth was dangerous, drinking water was lacking. As soon as land was cleared, seed was sown. No communication with the outside world was allowed, no correspondence. The Guru gradually exerted his hold over their being through an obedience automatically accepted. During the night, long hours of meditation broke down resistance. The heat was heavy, humid, the air filled with the barking of jackals.

In this effort, the novice lived torn between his dream of freedom and the body that had been brought back to where he no longer wished to be. His devotion was dying. He was absent from himself, lost. A nun who lived in the *âshram* upset him greatly. It was the first time he had spoken to a woman and this one was old enough to be his mother. One day she showed him the image of the *Ishtadevatâ* she was

---

[7] Kanya Kumarî, the fiancée whom Shiva forgot and who waits eternally for her beloved.

worshiping covered with flowers, and she said to him, "Just as I have put that beloved image in front of me to focus my concentration, I can also break it. At that moment, the Divine, if it pleases Him, can choose to enter into the heart and live there. You should know this and never forget it."

The Guru was anxious about the mental state of his favorite novice, who was escaping from him. He consulted several of the older ones about it. How could he bring back this rebel, whom he needed for his work, and attach him to the Guru for good? How could he prevent him from thinking? He decided to make him take the vows of continence on all levels (brah-mâcharya). Between the Guru and the novice the silence was broken, but the young man who had been brought back against his will resisted; the cocoon of paralyzing tenderness was torn. He asked, "What do you want from me? Where are you leading me?"

In this confrontation, both spoke openly—the Guru of attachment, the disciple of freedom. Finally the novice gave in before the power of the Master. The required vows were pronounced, but they included a condition: "I accept to work for you is full obedience, but let me not have cause to regret it later on. My path is the one which leads to the ultimate freedom."

Several years passed.

The handful of disciples who had followed the Swâmi to Assam had now increased to about fifty, making it necessary to create an autonomous institution. The property included the buildings where the monks and the novices lodged together with a few old couples and children of the lay disciples who were being brought up in the âshram. The âshram had its own school, a dispensary, a printing shop, weaving rooms, grain lofts, gardens, orchards, and rice fields. As time went on, the Swâmi who had been its creator had become, inevitably, an administrator, working day and night for the community. His urgent preoccupation—other groups having grown up in the nearby provinces—was to name his successor and have him recognized. The only one who was capable of taking over from him was his favorite novice, but would the latter, with his independent character and the aim he was pursuing, be likely to accept the *sannyâsa*[8] without which he could not be the head of a monastic institution?

The novice was working twenty hours a day, consumed by the tasks he was obliged to fulfill and by his thirst for the infinite. From time to time, an affectionate impulse made him break the silence and plead with his Master: "Stop, I implore you! Do not go on enlarging your work. You are getting caught in the net. Give it all up. You are being eaten up by your obligations. Return to inner life. Leave everything and do not look back! Go and sit under a tree in the forest and meditate. I will take care of you. I will go begging for you . . ." But the Guru, entirely identified with his work and its problems, could no longer detach himself. Then the disciple became more distressed: "I beg you to stop! The spirit of the *âshram* is dying. Each effort is useful in its way, but only up to a certain point. If the effort is maintained by will alone, it is no longer in tune with the natural rhythm of creation, and disintegration sets in."

The Master was quite aware of this, but to struggle against the established current had become impossible. The first impulse of the disciples, who had come to live in total renunciation, had little by little changed into unreasonable demands. In the course of the years, anniversary feasts had multiplied and all the poor came running to the *âshram* to be fed and clothed. Although the crowd flattered him, the Guru had no more illusions, even concerning the children, all sons of his

---

[8] Definite entrance into monastic life, with all the vows this entails.

nearest disciples, who had been entrusted to him by their parents so that they might grow up in the atmosphere of the *âshram*. He said, "It is possible that some of these children may open themselves to the light, but also that some of them may become thieves. In that case, they will be perfect thieves, because they are being fed and raised in the force, the energy and the sight of the Guru."

When the question of accepting *sannyâsa* was put to the novice, he asked for three days to think about it. For him *sannyâsa* was not only a formality that was needed in order to be put solemnly at the head of the *ashram*—for the salvation of the institution; it demanded a lifelong commitment of himself. In the course of the years that had gone by, he had blindly followed the rules established by the Guru: obedience, breaking from the family, poverty, continence, a constant discipline of the mind in order to attain an impersonal state—a kind of "little death" in which, if the stray impulses of the mind haven't given a wrong direction to the effort, true being could be born. But the aim was still the final freedom.

At the end of the first day of reflection, his heart torn between loyalty to the Guru who showed him such attachment and his own intense desire for freedom, the novice put a question to himself: "Does the required *sannyâsa* bind me inwardly?" The second day, he said to himself, "If I accept, I shall work in full obedience, but who will be responsible?" When he woke up on the third morning, he knew the answer: "Nobody and nothing can be binding on me. I am a Bâul. I am free." And so he said to the Guru, "Do whatever is useful for you. Inwardly, nothing can bind me."

The ceremony of his *sannyâsa* was very simple. According to the ancient Vedic tradition, the novice, calling the sun to witness, says three times: "I renounce, I renounce, I renounce." The Guru directed him to celebrate his own funeral service in order to burn his past. After that, the Master handed him the rough-hewn staff, the emblem of the monk, and prostrated himself before him. According to the law of the *Shastras*, they were now equals.

Symbolically, the new monk, Swâmi Nirvanânanda,[9] possessed nothing but a gourd (*kamandalou*) made from a dried fruit and his staff. But the Guru took the stick from him, saying, "If I do not take it from you, you will go off and will not do my work!" The new monk did not flinch. Although he was voluntarily bound to do his Guru's work, his mind remained free. Deliberately, at that very moment he made a vow that was to create an obstacle to the life of automatism that faced him: "The day the big tree at the *âshram* door disappears, in one way or another, that evening, I shall leave . . ."

More years passed, very hard ones.

The Guru had retired to Puri, and from there he traveled from city to city, always talking about the *âshram*, encouraging people who wished to go there and live. On this level, the *âshram* was a success; money flowed in. The old disciples busied themselves with settling in the newcomers.

Swâmi Nirvanânanda lived under greater and greater pressure with a load of obligations on his shoulders and, like Sinbad the Sailor with the Old Man of the Sea, he had to carry his Guru at the same time. One day he counted the number of years he had been working for the Guru, serving his human ambition, and felt free to leave. The *âshram* was prospering in its new direction. He was no longer necessary. He took his *kamandalou* and left. The same evening a violent storm tore down the tree at the door of the *âshram*.

But he felt miserable as he departed, for all opposition to the Guru had fallen away. Now he could but love him in his weaknesses with all the tenderness of bygone times. He felt

[9] "Joy-of-Realization-of-the-Void."

baffled, full of a grief which he knew would last for a certain time according to an exact law.

He vanished. He gave up his name.

The experience of death in oneself, which he had lived through little by little in the course of the years, accompanied him. He made his way to the Himalayas. At the end of his strength, he dragged himself to an *âshram* where wandering monks were received.

He remained there, on his rope bed, feverish, with no one to care for him. There is no mutual help among *sannyâsin*. If one of them dies, his body is burned or cast into the Ganges. How could there be room for pity in the vows of renunciation of oneself, since sooner or later all men have to throw off this used garment which the body represents? The miracle is to descend lucidly to the very last vibration of conscious life. That is the moment when a new birth can take place. One day in his weakness this man without identity saw a brilliant light before him and knew that he was not going to die. The ordeal was overcome.

He recovered, but he was no longer the same man. A long period of wandering began for him. He never speaks of those years. If questioned, a smile flits over his lips and he answers with a poetic phrase that leaves an aura of mystery. Friends told me of having met him in various places, although it was never possible to establish any chronological sequence in his travels or in the events of his life.

His former tenderness for Swâmi Nigamânanda remained the same. Although he had rebelled, he continued to serve his Guru by respecting his monastic vows and by devoting himself to the study of the *Vedas* which was to fill his life. They saw each other again only once, in Assam, and spoke openly about the divergent ways of the search for the self which had occasioned their parting. The disciple revealed himself in such a way that the Guru, blessing him, gave him full freedom to follow his solitary way. He had become an *atyâshramî*, one of those who are beyond all rules and all disciplines of an established order and who are recognized by the tradition.

With his long beard framing his thin face and in his white robe, he was sometimes taken for a Muslim *pîr*, sometimes for a Hindu *sâdhu*. For his part, he smiled at his freedom in a society full of taboos. He allowed a direct contact with people to take place, but at the same time he was like an empty shell filled with the sound of the ocean. I have heard him say, "What a strange experience. I cannot bind myself to anyone. They are in me, but I am not in them." This objectivity, so devastating in appearance, helped the growth of our work on ourselves with a merciless lucidity supported only by his look, amused and full of confidence.

One of his childhood friends once came across him in a northern city where, just for a bare living, he was preparing students for different university examinations. He had taken the name Anirvân. The professor in him was just another role voluntarily assumed. So, many hours a day, like a factory worker, he set himself to the work of translating the texts he considered necessary for the people who gathered around him once or twice a week. Soon other friends began meeting together in neighboring towns, each group organizing themselves so that his ticket from place to place could be paid and his visit assured.

The whole of life was his Guru and at the same time his field of action. He wrote to me once, "What people expect from me may not come about. All I can do is to be true to myself and sincere with others. I do my best not to hurt people, yet every one of our movements creates a reaction, however slight it may be. We cannot avoid it. All we can do is to accept this with good grace and without complicating things."

For him, any place was a good one in which to live an inner life and carry out one's task; even a room on a noisy street of a big city with electric lights burning day and night, the sounds of the market place, children shouting. The conditions under which he lived were extremely modest, difficult and complex, but he made light of them. He said, "If you walk for a long time carrying a burden on your shoulders, you get more and more tired, whereas the same burden will weigh nothing at all if you float it down a river. Is life not a river? My work also floats downstream. All my life, I have tried not to burden myself with cumbersome things. But how hard it is to live simply, not to amass things and thoughts. Of their own accord they pile up around you and in the end become a weight. At that point, one has to know how to slip between them like an eel and escape. One must never allow oneself to be caught."

For years, he has lived, and stayed for a while, only in those places where his freedom was completely respected. No one ever knows when he will go away, for he follows his own law, which is secret.

V

Everyday Life

One question bothered me: "How are we going to live together, we who are of such different backgrounds, with such
different customs?" My Hindu friends put it in their way:
"How are we going to bear our *karma* together?"[1] Then
Shrî Anirvân told us a story.

"In life, one has to know that one is at the same time the
cat who eats the mouse and the mouse who is eaten by the
cat, for life, as it comes to us and the life which is in us,
takes these two forms simultaneously. But can I understand
who I am if I do not know my place in the universe? When
this is seen, then I discover that the one who is first eaten is the
first to be liberated, while the other has a heavier *karma* to
bear. If I accept my responsibilities in the situation in which

[1] *Karma* is the occult force of *prakriti* (Great Nature) which brings
people together for some secret purpose.

I find myself, then the struggle or absence of struggle, in one way or the other, becomes the secret dignity of my inner being.

"The fervent disciple of a *sâdhu* went one day to beg in a village and there a peasant took a dislike to him and beat him with a stick. The disciple behaved according to his own understanding and did not hit back. On his way home, deeply immersed in himself, he forgot all about the peasant and the beating. But his Master saw the marks on his face and asked, 'What happened to you?' 'What?' asked the disciple. He could remember nothing. When the Master insisted, he searched in his memory and remembered what had taken place. 'And you didn't hit him back?' asked the Master. 'Why did you not share your aggressor's *karma?* Now go back and see what is going on because of you.' The disciple returned to the village, but from afar he saw flames. The house of the peasant who had beaten him was on fire."

Our life was made up of periods of work interrupted by periods of rest or of communal life. Each of us had his special task about which we did not speak among ourselves, for tacitly everything was related to that voluntary commitment. This gave flexibility to our relationship with one another. At the same time, my own solitude weighed on me, for in that "present" in which there was as yet no relief, I had no criterion to go by. Shrî Anirvân spoke to me about it as a potter might have spoken about a vase he was modeling. "Why not break it and begin over again? In that case, one has again to knead the clay, soften it with water, and begin from scratch." I accepted inner work interpreted in that way. What kind of clay was I? Constant, minute observation of myself was beginning, though I did not know where I was going—but I had complete trust in the potter.

The evening meal—always the same—milk, boiled potatoes,

butter, salt, and sugar—brought us all together. The food was just food and not meant as a diversion for the eyes or greedy taste. After a day of individual work and concentration, we enjoyed an open conversation, speaking about our experiences, about our difficulties with ourselves. Shrî Anirvân listened to us with patience. "In a ground that has not been plowed for a long time, one cannot sow wheat right away," he would say. "We are at the stage of preparing the ground. Various crops must be sown and plowed back into the soil to make it fertile."

In the evening, when Shrî Anirvân came back from his walk, and if there were no visitor announced for a private interview, the hour belonged to me. Outside, nightfall—the moment when the crows made great circles in the sky. We used to speak about the little facts of our lives and of my life, for all these details began to have a meaning related to a reality that still escaped me.

For several weeks a young Hindu woman came to give me lessons in Hindi. She had a degree. A servant came with her and waited for her, stretched out like a lizard in the sun. My tutor took me through a real course on the *Râmâyana*, at the same time explaining her profound contempt for foreigners. To her I was not a foreigner. I listened, apparently without reacting, putting my hand over my mouth, as Hindu women do to hide any expression. One day she announced that she was leaving me, for a reason which was only a pretext: a relation's marriage in some far-off province.

Another incident: The village woman who came to cut the grass on the terraces used to steal lemons from the neighboring gardens in order to make me an offering. One blow with her sickle and the fruit fell into the skirt held up to receive it! She explained, "You are my mother, God makes the fruit grow, and I pick it, for you."

The peasant who regularly brought me his rice from the

village, used to sing at the top of his voice: *"Jaï, Jaï Sîtâ-Râm, Jaï, Jaï . . ."* like an automaton, happy in his poverty, absorbed in his song. My "weekly" beggar woman, who came on Mondays for a day's food, used to stroke my shoulder as if I were her sister. Both of them spoke to me about the "golden breast of our Divine Mother."[2] "Ah, yes," Shrî Anirvân explained, "these simple people get food from the essence of the spirit which for them quite naturally takes on density in matter. This idea is far more ancient than any philosophical idea of power assuming a form. In the *Vedas*, the earth is not yet heavy matter. It is spirit and from its essence the Divine Mother is born. Simple people have not forgotten this, for their chemistry is nearer to the truth than ours, therefore they are better nourished than we."

One evening, while we were talking, a voice was heard far away singing, *"Namah Shivâya . . .* [O Shiva, I prostrate myself before thee]" on two low notes, a *re* and a *mi* a quarter tone lower. The rhythm was that of a quick march. The invocation came nearer and nearer, louder and louder as it approached the house, then faded away in the forest. An echo carried it back for a long time. Shrî Anirvân said, "A great sacrifice has been offered up."

The chant of the priests who accompany the dead to the cremation ground is quick and hard. One hears it from a distance in the mountains, for the way down to the River Koshî is long. A little group of men go by at a run, with the body on an uncovered litter on their shoulders. Their chant runs with them through the dust, in time with their steps, in time with their breathing. The voices are guttural:

> *Ram Nam satya he*
> *Satya bolo gatta he.*
> [The Name of Râma is truth,
> Revealed truth is liberation.]

[2] *Hiranyavakshâ aditi.*

Once a week in the afternoon, Shrî Anirvân received three of the town notables, very old men. Their heads were shaven except for one lock on the top and a fringe of white beard. They carried knobbed walking sticks. They came to read aloud an *Upanishad*. Shrî Anirvân gave a commentary on each verse, which became for them the support of their thought in the following days. The text was chanted in Sanskrit, the commentary given in Hindi. The three men would sit facing Shrî Anirvân. I had the right to sit on a cushion a little to the rear. If I did not understand what was said, I could see in their eyes what they were receiving; felt in myself the immobility of their bodies, their inner silence which allowed the Being to open. All my attention was focused on approaching this quietness in my disobedient body and vagabond thoughts. When the lesson had come to an end and our guests had risen, I saluted them by "taking the dust from under their feet." They would then make a sign of parting and blessing, a little hesitant since I was a stranger. Shrî Anirvân, unperturbed, looked on with love in his eyes.

One day only two of them came. After the lesson, Shrî Anirvân told me: "Our missing friend died two days ago. One morning he saw the hand of death (*Yama*) coming towards him. He understood the sacred sign and took leave of each of the members of his family; then he went up alone onto the hill, forbidding anyone to follow him. He sat under a tree and tied himself to the trunk with his shawl. He cut off his topknot of hair and placed it in front of him, with all he had on him—his watch, his wallet—all the while reciting the prayers which made him a monk. Then, gazing straight before him, he recited the prayers of consecration. When his eldest son found him, he had been dead for several hours. Each of us may well wish for a death like that in full self-consciousness."

Among us, the pupils, the atmosphere was not always so

relaxed as it could have been. One of the Bengali women having been allowed to cook a special dish, there followed a series of special dishes in competition, a reaction to the moderation that was demanded of us. Shrî Anirvân liked extreme simplicity. Food should be considered merely as material used for nourishing the spirit. The first mouthful of rice was raised to the forehead in salutation; some verses from the *Bhagavad Gîtâ* were recited mentally with the next four mouthfuls.

Sometimes criticisms were exchanged among us, and there were moments of impatience disguised by extreme politeness. I often felt myself walled in, in a heavy body with no life in it other than an intense pain. And the others—what was going on in them? Their presence reassured and irritated me at the same time. I knew that if I had said, "I shall never reach anything," Shrî Anirvân would have reminded me of a certain Puranic story:

"Some devotees in a mango orchard were talking among themselves. Each one knew the kind of mango which grew in his province. Soon they began to count the different varieties of trees in the orchard and in the end began to quarrel about the way they should be grown. Suddenly the owner of the orchard arrived and, much surprised, said to them, 'Why do you not eat this beautiful ripe fruit hanging on the branches instead of counting the leaves on the trees?'"

VI

Study

I often heard our visitors ask Shrî Anirvân, "Why do you not publish your teaching?" and his answer was "At the time of the *Vedas*, the Master spent many years giving instruction to the 'chosen man' to whom he would transmit the spiritual knowledge he possessed. Nowadays, because of printing and communications facilities, spiritual science has become an affair of the market place. If one considers the march of time, it is just as important to talk to trees as to talk to men, for the tree and man are both part of Great Nature. The sage has to work in harmony with the slow evolutionary transformation, without concern for the enormous waste it entails. When Shrî Aurobindo speaks of the transformation of species, he is looking into the future. In fact, the passage from one species to another takes millions of years; during that time the sage is responsible for the survival of the vital spirit."

Shrî Anirvân sometimes gave us to understand that he was "doing his time in the Himalayas" to be in communion with the earth which prays. The earth prays; it leads people to wish to know the mystery of the Void. Just as one always returns to the fundamental teaching of Patanjalî,[1] so one day he would return to Assam and Bengal. He said, "My ambition is not very great. It is to live a life rich in impressions, luminous to the end; to leave behind a few books embodying my life-long search for truth, and a few souls who have caught fire. My aim? Simply to inspire people, and give them the most complete freedom to live their own life. No glamour, no fame, no institution—nothing. To live simply and die luminously."

For many years he had been working under a yoke without losing his freedom. "Work does not find me," he said, "because I never search for it. If it is thrust upon me, I devote all my energy to it and then when it is taken away, I never look back. Once it is done, I forget it, for the only thing I care for is the idea that 'I am'—that idea is at once an in-dividual, a cosmic and transcendental law in itself."

When Muslims looked at him, they asked, "Is he one of us?" Some Hindus, not yet freed from form, would question him. Then Shrî Anirvân very humbly explained: "I must tell you that I never wore the ocher robe of my own free will. It was put on me by my Guru, who attached great importance to everything that had to do with the idea of institution. He himself always dressed elegantly, like a man of the world. It is true that this robe never had much meaning for me and that is why I discarded it one day as easily as I had put it on."

I did not yet know all the methods that Shri Anirvan used in order to test us. One day a group of ocher-robed monks, the most distinguished of a well-known monastery, came to visit us. They were curious to see a Cultural Center in proc-

[1] The author of the *Yoga-Sûtras*, who probably lived in the second century B.C.

ess of formation where, under different forms, the inner experience was recognized as identical in substance. One of the monks asked me casually, "But, if I am not mistaken, this must be where Shrî Anirvân lives?"

This was in the morning. Nobody ever disturbed Shrî Anirvân at that hour. Nevertheless, I went and knocked on his door. Surprised, he asked me, "Do you personally wish that I should come?—Yes? Then in a few minutes."

When I went back to the monks on the veranda, they had embarked on a very learned philosophical discussion while eating the fruit that had been served to them. In a little while Shrî Anirvân appeared and, like an anonymous mendicant, sat on a stool to one side, his scarf wrapped around his face. He looked so pitiful that the discourse continued and nobody paid any attention to him. After ten minutes Shrî Anirvân asked me in a low voice: "Do you agree that I can go away?" He got up and left discreetly. The monks had not stopped talking. That evening, at the study hour, I was still blushing.

On the occasion of the visit of some friends of Shrî Anirvân from Allahabad, we had the "class" at an unusual hour. A white sheet spread out on the floor of the library marked the space where we sat together. Twelve years later, I still have a mental picture of our group: three women in white sarîs with red borders, five or six men of different ages, among whom were two lawyers and a doctor in a long buttoned frock coat with a white cap on his head. Nobody took notes.

Shrî Anirvân had put the following question: "What is the function of the interiorization of consciousness?"

On this occasion he said, "The too-facile affirmation that man is spirit but born of the flesh needs some sort of introduction. Every religion makes a distinction from the start between the natural man and the spiritual man, which is the reason for the great importance given to a sacrament marking the passage from the one state to the other. This sacrament has a social significance; in Aryan society, it formally admits the child to partaking in the spiritual heritage of the community, or else it can also remain secret; but it is always a bond, like the reins that in a visible way link the horse with the coachman of the symbolic team described in the *Katha Upanishad*.[2] Our attention needs to be directed to the factors that make it possible to approach the individual sacrament (*diksha*), for it is in fact the actual commitment to a particular spiritual discipline. Such a commitment is voluntary; it is the 'setting forth' on the spiritual adventure with no possibility of return.

"But this all-important moment which separates the natural man from the spiritual man also separates vital values from spiritual values in an artificial manner, whereas conscious evolution is nothing but a process of inner continuity, strangely similar to the growth of a seed. For the young plant to open out, an atmosphere composed of two categories of values is absolutely necessary. While favorable surroundings can modify the vital values so that the latter may better reflect the mind, a training is necessary before the mind is able to control and utilize properly the vital values. A broadening of thought can be observed chronologically. In the *Vedas*, the word '*karma*' designated only spiritual work, while the *Bhagavad Gîtâ* spiritualizes all forms of activity, including the unconscious and psychological movements of life. It then becomes a question not only of a rise in level, but also of a deepening and widening of consciousness, which is the aim of spirituality. There is no divorce between the aim of spirituality and the aim of life, which is growth. Spiritual search is a conscious effort to grow by harmonious assimilation and at the same time an intensification of consciousness.

[2] I.3.3.-4

"But how many steps to climb! As soon as we have set out on the way, we try to spiritualize every instant of our life in a conscious or unconscious manner. Should the unconscious effort be supported by favorable social conditions or by a rudimentary inner need, it is already a preparation for a conscious effort, for the entire process depends on the dynamism of consciousness in search of clarity. Indeed, a sort of clarity comes as soon as the sensory values of animal life begin to be transformed into values of the understanding. The power to handle ideas is a conquest of consciousness. But though sensations may be clear and precise, the way they are understood by one person and another are very different. Sensations, even badly interpreted, are the only instrument a man possesses at the beginning of his search to put an order into his experiences, to shape his way of life, and to discover the laws of Great Nature.

"On this level, the repetition of experiences related to the senses gives him a power of control. It is a help for creating his own inner world, although the values of this still only derive from outer influences. In the long run, this position is discovered to be false, for particular facts, even held to be true, still belong to the world of the senses. And the crucial point in the problem, paradoxically, is to grasp the universal on the ideal plane in order to project it onto the particular. Such is the pivot on which the spiritual effort turns: to transform the given values to the point where consciousness becomes dynamically free in its enjoyment of the 'I.' It is here that the interiorization of consciousness comes into play. This is the inescapable first step to be made. One of the *Rishis* of the *Upanishads* clearly formulated its law: 'Pure Existence (*Sat*) pierces an opening to project itself into the phenomenal world.'[3] Human consciousness obeys the same law, but the result is a degradation and a blunting of the conscious energy.

[3] *Chhândogya Up.* 6.8.4.

To maintain the fire of life within it, the process has to be reversed."

And Shrî Anirvân said further:

"If formulated in an abstract way, the call to observe oneself seems fantastic and even alarming at the beginning, yet to look into the depths of oneself is a necessary stage in the evolution of consciousness. Since it is an aim to be pursued in everyday life, the way of going about it must be clear and all the possibilities foreseen. What is more, it must be known that a certain quality of imagination will necessarily be utilized by the thought. In other words, it is necessary to 'imagine'[4] what pure thought will be and to know at the same time that pure thought will only arise when the habitual automatism of thought is suspended. The same applies to our life, when in the midst of our occupations, a temporary and voluntary suspension of all activity is necessary to clarify our consciousness. Even if that moment is very short, consciousness will discern, in a flash of perception, what comes from the outer world and what from the inner world. But to exert any control whatsoever, one must first of all be able to control one's own thoughts. Therefore a control dictated from outside—let us call it a voluntary discipline—must play its role until the inner being is revealed."

Another evening, Shrî Anirvân sketched for us a picture of the development of independent thought in India in order to lead up to the question of the Bâüls and the Sufis. "Modern India," he told us, "follows intellectually a philosophical religion which is composed for the most part of *Sâmkhya*[5] with a little *Vedanta*. Every cultured person knows it. In this connection, the word 'Hinduism'—rather vague and broad—can include and satisfy every curiosity. But what is tragic is

[4] Based on a knowledge of what is real.
[5] See p. 92.

that cultured society, from the time of the *Upanishads*, has completely turned away from the religion of the people. Popular beliefs, in their Tantric forms, with a background of Vedism, are intentionally ignored and the Hindu monks who teach *Vedanta* in Europe and in America, by tacit agreement amongst themselves, keep silent on the subject.

"In their family life, the people follow the autochthonous religion which the Aryans found in India when they arrived, an essentially practical religion far from any written teaching. This religion, still very alive, is founded on the close relationship existing between woman who embodies the power of *Shakti*[6] and the earth. Though this cult of the woman was not formulated in a particular philosophy, it breathed life into all the philosophies, which without it would have lacked all radiance. It gives name and form (*nama-rupa*) to the power of the primordial energy, so that the believers of all faiths can apprehend it. The greatly worshiped 'Divine Mother' was born and made incarnate to pour forth forever her grace and blessings on those who call upon her. The Divine Mother made her way into the temples, took her seat on private altars, was enclosed in amulets. She accepted a thousand names and forms, for an abstract symbol is not sufficient, anywhere, to nourish the heart. For those who worshiped her, she became the outlet for their strength, their passion, their despair, and their tenderness.

"On their arrival in India, the Vedic Aryans, who formed the aristocracy of priests and warriors, worshiped the spiritual principle 'sunlit life' in a ritual that was far beyond the understanding of the aborigines. So that they also might worship the sun, but on their level, the simple people merely gave human features to the sun—who became Vishnu-the-Radiant. This was a spontaneous concretization. It followed, histori-

[6] The primordial energy, the conscious force of the Divinity, the Divine in action, the feminine aspect of the One.

cally, that one of the Vedic princes, Krishna, who would
never accept the throne even though it was his by right,
espoused the cause of the people and denounced the rituals
and sacrifices from which he was excluded.[7] Certainly he
wished to be free, but without ever himself becoming the
sannyâsin whose spirit and form he praised in the *Bhagavad
Gîtâ*.[8] Because of this, Krishna personified forever the 'way
to liberation' for all the oppressed and became for them the
All-Powerful-Divine-Lord. For a long time before the story
of Krishna was written down, it was passed on by oral tradition. He is represented as having been taken by force from his
royal surroundings and brought up by villagers. He is above
all else the Child-God playing with the *gopis*[9] and, in the
Bhagavad Gîtâ, the Lord who teaches. His greatness lies in
having transformed daily existence, with all its sufferings, into
sacrifices for love. Thanks to him, the poorest man, though
hungry, plays his flute and sings his love without complaint."

Another evening, we took up again the question: "What
are the forms of pre-Vedic religions that give life to India?"

"They are very much intermingled," said Shrî Anirvân.
"The generally accepted idea that everything Vedic belongs
exclusively to the Aryan culture does not mean that everything Aryan is Vedic, for as soon as the Aryans arrived in
India, some of them refused to submit to the authority of the
Vedas and were persecuted. These heretical Aryans, driven
out as though they had been undesirable nomads, went away
and settled on the eastern boundaries with their free thought,
their democratic way of life, without gods, without kings,
without castes. If we look back to these beginnings, it is because they show how independent thought has been literally

---

[7] Kings belong to the second caste, the Kshatriyas.

[8] 6, 1. The *Bhagavad Gîtâ* is only one of the scriptures containing a
wealth of practical spiritual instructions.

[9] The shepherdesses.

suppressed in India since Vedic times. Secretly, however, it became the great 'subterranean current' of force that inspires us, causing flames of living spirituality to spring up here and there;[10] these flames are extinguished at a given moment only to blaze up again, later and elsewhere, with equal strength.

"Here we come to the history of the well-known rebels, independent souls, which is at the same time the history of the great Gurus. They are known in history under the name *Vratyas*[11] and are only spoken of with contempt! With the passing of time, silence fell on the subject of this minority who had dared to defy the fierce Vedic orthodoxy. If the *Vratyas* are mentioned in some of the writings, it is always in harsh terms: 'They are the ones who, without having been initiated into the Vedic cult, speak as though they had been . . . they are the ones who claim to play the Guru without being Gurus . . .'

"Although the *Vratyas* did not observe the Vedic forms of worship, they believed in a great Being who can be described only negatively; here we recognize Shiva:

> . . . in the beginning there was the One.
> From Him everything emanated.
> he who knows this *Vratya*
> is called *vidvan vratya* . . .

"Very soon this great Being, free from all slavery, became the prototype of the living, liberated man, of the Shivaite monk completely indifferent to Vedic orthodoxy. This wandering monk, roaming about naked, his body smeared with ashes, possessing nothing but his gourd, so impressed the people that he soon occupied the foreground, leaving the priests far behind.

"Another wanderer, equally free from all social rules, ap-

[10] Shrî Râmana Maharshi is a striking example.
[11] They are often described as "the savage hordes."

peared at about the same time—the Bâûl, a counterpart of the
'Man in the heart,' of an inner state which can be attained
only by personal discipline. Since the Bâûls did not recognize
caste distinction, since they had no temple, worshiped no God
and made no pilgrimages to sacred places, they were considered to be rebels. As soon as India was invaded by Islam,[13]
Sufis of all lines of descent joined with them. They became
like one family, singing the same songs, playing the same instrument. Together they followed the same precepts: to submit to and obey the 'Man seated in the temple of the heart,' to
respect the secrets of others, to use money simply and without attachment, to expend themselves for the good of others,
to show themselves strong with the strong and humble before
the weak."

The Sufi who was among our guests said, "What I am I do
not know. If you have a Guru, you have no more head,
but only *fana*, that sensation of infinite expansion which is the
Void. Your intuition is fed by the immensity of the Guru's
intuition. I absorb what he gives me, 'I am,' until I am filled
to overflowing. It is not I who have touched the Guru's
coat, it is he who holds me by the hand."

> The Bâûl travels in the Void
> in which all voices resound
> O Bhagavan . . .

[12] The *Shaiva* represents the *Purusha* aspect and the Bâûl the *prakriti*
aspect of the same spiritual discipline.
[13] In the eleventh century.

VII

Problems

The Brahmins who gravitated around us lived for the most part in Almora and were lawyers. They took time to visit each other, smoked water pipes together, and conversed on matters to do with God, the temple, and the priesthood, as well as on those concerning their large families, the town, and the land. Each of them had two or three disciples (*chelas*) attached to their person to carry out all their wishes—to carry a message, to write letters, or quite simply to keep them company. These were young men of the same caste learning to play their role in society, or some distant relative of the family, or students in charge of the children's education.

Our friends were all orthodox. My relationship with them was excellent because as one who was serving Shrî Anirvân, I had a recognized status. While I observed all their rules of conduct, I also imposed my own rules when they came to visit Haïmavatî. "Be careful," Shrî Anirvân warned me. "They will forgive your failure to keep the rules of others, but they will not be tolerant if you fail to obey your own!" My rules had to do with the practical facts of life at Haïmavatî. The stone flags in the rooms were washed every morning. No garbage such as fruit peelings was to be thrown in the garden. I asked the women not to dry their washing on the bushes, the stairs, or the roof. These demands, minimal from my point of view, went against habits and raised a conflict in myself. The rule I imposed on myself was never to ask a question and never to ask a favor.

There were difficult moments when I felt far removed from my own culture and yet unable to understand the customs of the people around me. With Shrî Anirvân I never reacted in this way for he had the art of making me live from my own substance and not from his; he gave me the strength not to be weak with myself. With my Hindu friends, I looked for the point of contact where direct communication could take place. We spoke about the same efforts, but we did not have the same reactions. Certainly I succeeded in mastering my own, and in this way I learned a great many things about myself. I did what was expected of me, I said the words that were supposed to be said, but when I went back to my room, I asked myself, "What am I doing here?" And my answer to myself was "You are watching yourself live!" It was impossible to cheat, for there was no one to approve or disapprove of anything I did; there was only "me" becoming my own obstacle. And the game was worth playing.

The isolation in which we lived finally created a curious phenomenon. It was as though a cloak of mist distorted the outlines of things and transformed the abstract values of what we were looking for. Whereas Shrî Anirvân had always spoken about the harmonizing of the ego within the radiant being, we began to get lost in talk about "the destruction of the ego."

The psychological poverty of my Hindu friends was con-
cealed within an exaggerated sense of their own importance.
In fact they were imprisoned by caste, family customs, and
life routine. The direct consequence of this state of things
was a continuous dream described in a cosmic vocabulary
and used as an escape from life. Such was one of the many
problems brought to Haïmavatî and laid before "the one who
knew" so that he might direct the mind towards another dimension. The great difficulty was passivity. Many begged
for the Master's blessing and wished to live in his orbit, for it
is easier to exist in his shadow, to watch him live, to rejoice in
his asceticism, than to struggle oneself. A process of dissolution (*pralaya*) gave a glimpse that one is far closer to God in
death than in life. Subconsciously, each one wished to die or
retire from the world, to "get out of it," no longer to bear
the weight of it. To leave everyday life for the sake of finding something else—a stability around an impersonal axis—
meant an almost superhuman effort in this land which had become a museum of rites. But if this effort were directed
towards action and towards the liberation of the self, a solu-
tion could be found without having to destroy the ego.

Shrî Anirvân said, "If you truly wish to see your conditions as they are, you must realize that from childhood on,
even with a highly developed intelligence, you have no chance
of making a choice in the circumstances of your life. You
grow up in a hierarchic order, your career is predetermined,
you are given the wife with whom you will make your
earthly journey. These conditions of respect and obedience
are ideal for being completely free in spirit. Great Nature
allows nothing to escape from her. Repetition exists on all
levels: movement, attitudes, speech follow a known gradation
which ensures the continuation of the species in the same
pattern. The centripetal law is allowed full play.

"But where is this freedom to which you aspire? It has to

be paid for dearly. The *âshram* life which appeals to you is only family life transposed into a broader frame. The Guru is the father, the *Gurupatnî* is the mother, with all her prerogatives. The change in the pattern would only be in the orientation of your vocabulary bondage towards a movement rising in a spiral, around an axis which goes from the nadir to the zenith."

The Europeans among us found the solitude hard to bear. Any physical effort required at that high altitude[1] and in the tropics, combined with the anguish aroused by the strangeness of the landscape, created a certain tension. Unlike the Hindus, the freedom of the Europeans to accept or to destroy all the elements of their private life, including even their stay at Haïmavatî, aroused a whole range of emotions. At a certain time, the body, having accepted new habits which were often uncomfortable, reacted violently. Our guests would escape into the forest for long hours at a time on non-existent pretexts: some dry wood to pick up, a new path to be discovered, a lost sandal . . . they would come back with explanations that nobody was asking for. The Hindus, more accustomed to communal life and to the tensions of the inner life, merely said, "I am at my saturation point," and with a slowing-down equal to the eagerness of the first days, they would allow themselves long periods of retirement. Shrî Anirvân let it all go on. Everybody was suffering in one way or another, like an iron bar when it is thrown into the fire and then beaten on the anvil to give it the required shape.

As for me, my task was to be "alone" in the midst of civilities, offerings, demands, and ironies. Did our guests have any idea that my heart very often bled to see their inner hunger? In the evening, in front of Shrî Anirvân, it was my turn to beg and plead until he made the little movement of his head

---

[1] About 7,200 feet.

that meant it was time to get up and go away. We were all playing a game under pressure.

Traditional techniques affirm that although one cannot change one's character, one can nevertheless become free from it by making it sufficiently supple. What remains at that point is not a residue, but the very foundation of being, stripped bare. If this basis were to disappear, it would be death. "One must have experienced the process," Shrî Anirvân used to say, "before undertaking a more advanced discipline. To fashion a gold ring, the jeweler uses pure gold and an alloy. He is a smelter when he works in the descending movement, an artist-engraver in the ascending movement. He is liberated only when he sells his jewel. It would be madness to believe in a possible liberation without having voluntarily descended many, many times to the foundation of being, to know the mysterious seed in us where the life of Great Nature is hidden."

One of our guests, a man of sixty-five who was a lawyer, spoke to me of the daily discipline he tried to follow. For several years he tried consciously to limit all his desires to three major principles:

—to try to live fully in the present moment which fills all space and time;

—not to give more importance to transitory happenings than to a monsoon rain which falls violently and may stop at any moment;

—not to waste time on things that are outside immediate concern.

The fact that he consciously refused to let himself be drawn into what did not concern him meant not interfering in the fate of other people. In life, this man was like all

others; but face to face with himself he evaluated his resistance to the current of life. When he came to the *âshram,*
his questions to Shrî Anirvân, even more than the answers,
showed him the direction to follow. "How," he said, "can
one ask a question which is true from the beginning to the
end?"

We received the news that S., a friend of Shrî Anirvân, died
in Delhi. He left a wife, five children, and parents who were
dependent on him. Nobody ever knew who he was. In the
family group he lived according to the consciousness of the
group and made it a discipline of introspection from which he
derived all that he gave to those around him. Shrî Anirvân said
often, "He knew how inwardly to create the solitude that is
propitious for divine delights. He has gone away with his
secret."

The Hindu women who came to Haïmavatî felt quite at
home after a few days, even though they had to give up the
habit of drying their washing all over the place! They spoke
a mixture of Hindi and Pahari, the dialect of the mountains,
which I found difficult to follow. I had to discover by myself
the depth of their spiritual quest, all that they knew and how
they were the cloak of nothingness which the men threw
over their shoulders. My life as a Western woman, my work,
my travels did not interest them. I could easily have appeared
for them as a professional storyteller!

Their world seemed to me at first to be very small, but
soon I became interested in their devotions and discovered
how the Brahman, nameless and formless in manifestation, in-
terpenetrates life in an active way, makes everything the
senses allow us to perceive divine: the wind, a perfume, a
song, a tree, a fruit, an animal, and particularly the husband
and the child. Anything could become the logical support
leading to the undifferentiated Divine. While the men had
spoken to me of the *Vedanta* philosophy, unconnected with

everyday life, the women, through the *Tantras*, perceived every single thing as animate. In the mountains, the gods have no sculptured image. The stone cup placed on top of the little square temples represents the being who offers himself to heaven to receive grace, rain, abundance. In the shade, big pebbles marked with a red dot hold the power that unites heaven and earth. Each woman had in her shrine a little of the sacred earth of Badrinath and Kedarnath, the two temples from which one makes the ascent to heaven.

The first time I was invited to step over the wall of orthodoxy of a Brahmin family in Almora was on the third birthday of a little boy. For the occasion the women of the two families, the Pants and the Joshis, were wearing a special shawl on which was painted the emblem of their clan (*gotra*). The glittering of the many feast-day sarîs looked as if the house were flowing with gold. Traditional hospitality required my hosts to receive me as though the Divine had knocked at their door and at the same time the caste laws forbade that I should eat with them! To save the situation a compromise was found. While the grandmothers, the aunts, and the widows were watching the child being blessed by the priests, the younger women watched me eat alone like a princess surrounded by her court. Then they led me by force into the presence of the goddess of the house, who was also draped in the shawl of the clan. A joyful impulsive curiosity kept us all close together until it was time for me to leave just before sunset. I could not be late. Shrî Anirvân's disciple had to be home before nightfall.

Whenever I went out from Haïmavatî, I never failed to meet *sâdhus* on the road. Their life intrigued me. They went by, carried forward by their vision, begging their pittance though often ill-received in the poor valleys. Some of them had a definite itinerary; others, like dead leaves, were blown by the wind from place to place. All obeyed alike the same rule: not to stay more than three nights under the same roof. Some of them had the bearing of princes in disguise, others were ragged or had their body smeared with ashes. Whoever they were, with their beautiful names—"Abandonment-in-God," "Joy-in-Austerity," "Pure-Vision-of-the-Infinite"—they had the tradition with them, for the renunciation, of which they were the living symbol, was envied by many. They were part of the totality of the anonymous efforts by which the mass is leavened. In a word, their search and mine were somewhat the same.

Higher knowledge is certainly not to be picked up on the trails in the Himalayas, nor yet is it hidden in the caves; but it exists for the few, for those at the stage of direct perception. One evening, we translated from Kabir a few lines from a text written half in Urdu, half in Hindi:

The *Purânas* and the *Koran* are only words
but behind the veil of the words, I see . . .

The water in the *ghats*[2] is cold, the Gods are mute,
but I, Kabir, am hot-blooded and I have a tongue . . .

[2] The stony bank of a river where ablutions are performed.

VIII

Lessons from Life

Our young servant was called Prem (which means "divine love"). It was the first time he had served in a house where there was a foreigner. Though quite unaware of it, Prem was destined to be my teacher in many realms. Shrî Anirvân never gave orders—a sign, a look was enough. He was always served first. I gave orders, but they would not be carried out unless they were given indirectly since Prem belonged to a high caste. It was up to me to know what he would never do, and make arrangements accordingly.

Prem, the passive witness of all that went on, managed very cleverly to be always respectful and contemptuous at the same time. Barefoot on the stone slabs, he came and went inaudibly with an absent-minded air. In the evenings he lit the oil lamps and went to sit on a wall in the garden. Soon the sound of his flute would be heard. He could neither read nor write, but he was good at sums! His mistakes in arithmetic were just little tricks tried out to see whether I was a real mistress or not. His sleepy mind irritated me. Shrî Anirvân said one day, "Well, then, teach him to think! In a few years Prem will perhaps own a tea shop and be a member of the village council!"

Prem tolerated the wildcat I had brought from Lohaghat. She followed me about everywhere, but allowed no one to touch her. Shrî Anirvân often said, "Pussy is your disciple. You are responsible for her. She is a perfect cat, who shows it by doing her own cat business very well." In the evening she used to come into the room where we were talking and take up her position in front of a hole between the stone slabs and the outer wall. She would stay on guard there for hours without moving. She knew perfectly well that sooner or later a rat would come through the hole because there were no other holes and plenty of foolhardy young rats! When one did come, she was ready. No struggle, no playing about. One snap and her teeth were in the back of his neck. She then threw him into the air to break his spine, exactly as a panther deals with his prey. "Are you as vigilant and watchful as Pussy?" asked Shrî Anirvân.

This cat provoked an incident with Prem that had a great effect on my behavior. I had bought a drinking glass in town for a flower vase. One day Prem poured boiling water into it and it cracked. Prem said, "It is Pussy's fault." I answered back, "Liar!" and there was anger in my voice. I looked up and saw Shrî Anirvân on the doorstep. I felt I had been caught doing wrong without knowing why. Nothing was said in front of Prem, but in the evening the Master said, "It was you who were wrong in answering like that. When you have found out and understood why, we will speak about it."

Six years later the question came up again when I was

visiting Shrî Anirvân in Shillong and we were talking about impressions received from our surroundings.

"Do you remember Prem?" he asked. "You two were obeying different laws. The influences around him were too different for him to understand them. He was never sure of approval and so he was slow in everything he did to have time to affirm himself, to have confidence in his reactions. In his own eyes he could not make a blunder—what would he have explained to his family? In front of something incomprehensible, isn't the simplest thing to accuse the other? Don't we do it all the time because we don't trust our reactions? Prem asked himself no questions, his life was a series of impulses, while your Pussy was perfectly in harmony with the laws of her nature. Our reactions are fed by the laws we recognize and they in turn lead us back to the great cosmic law."

Several of us went one evening to hear a sacred chant (*kirtan*) led by Nârâyan Mahâraj.[1] Seated in the lotus posture, Nârâyan was as beautiful as a young god. He was about forty. His face, without a wrinkle, was framed in black curls. His shawl, draped over one shoulder, left his breast bare. A necklace of crystal beads and *rudrâkshas*[2] signified life-death, Tantrism, and Shivaism. He accompanied the chant with *taraks*, a kind of castanet. The rhythm died away under his hands, only to come to life again without a pause. Little by little the sacred ectasy began; the movement of his right arm wrapped the fullness of his voice around him, his shoulders swayed from right to left. Nârâyan was like a tree bending to the storm. He sang a sacred word, a *mantra*, which was repeated by his audience in the same tenuous, vibrant rhythm. Feeling was at its peak.

This went on for a long time. And then, quite suddenly,

---

[1] Shrî Nârâyan Swâmi of Soosa, died around 1958.
[2] Seed of a fruit.

Nârâyan was silent. In the abrupt stillness, he stayed with his arms uplifted, his body rigid, living an emotion he communicated to us. His face reflected an intense joy . . . then, slowly, he came back to himself, murmuring as if to the gods, his body relaxed. His *taraks* had slipped to one side. Earlier, the skin of one of the drums had burst and at that moment his face had reflected intense pain. Something had broken. Then he had gone on with his song.

I did not recognize myself in those moments of shared exaltation. Later, I asked, "Who is Nârâyan?"

"He is a great artist," said Shrî Anirvân. "His song fills him. It is astonishing to follow his movement around the axis of the body. He is as supple as the seaweed in the sea; he gives the impression of being transparent, full of light. Has he been feeding on milk and honey? He sucks in the atmosphere around him and swallows three-quarters of it to feed the sap of his ascending force. The remaining quarter is for whoever happens to be ready to take it. A pure being like Nârâyan— the least sexual desire would kill him—feeds the soul of those around him for a long time. He brings a warm sensation which leaves a recognizable taste. But as soon as the mind begins to play with it, all that is fundamentally primitive in such adoration is spoiled. Reason condemns it and drives it out; then adoration comes in by the back door and becomes worship of movie stars, of a life of luxury, of sex.

"Tagore used to invite Bâüls and Sufis to chant *kirtans* at his house. Many of his poems were born in such an atmosphere. Shrî Râmakrishna experienced ecstasies of the same kind and his great disciple, Swâmi Vivekânanda, was one of the greatest *sankirtanists* of his time, though in the West he never spoke of it for fear of criticism. In orthodox Islam, too, there are those who break down the barriers, like Raihana Tyabji, the *pîr* of Kanpur, and others. For them, *bhâva* and *fana* are words which reveal exactly the same creative joy."

Years later, Shrî Anirvân used the same words—*bhâva, fana*—when he said, "Râmana Maharshi was like the trunk of a tree, the *pîr* of Kanpur like its foliage, Nârâyan like its flowers. The one drew sap from the earth, the second was a breathing in of life-giving air, the third was the perfume of flowers. But they were all fed from one and the same root. What can a Master truly do for his disciples? He can do no more than create the phenomenon which breaks down resistances and invade by surprise the soul of the one who opens to him—this is the only possible way."

That same evening Shrî Anirvân told me the story of a Hindu woman who was to arrive the next day. Her name was Pushpa. Her story began on the day the River Damodar rose furiously out of its bed, carrying everything with it. There were many deaths. Hundreds of villages were destroyed before the waters became calm and the flooded land reflected the clouds passing overhead.

Shrî Anirvân continued: "My Guru opened a camp to take in the victims of the flood and sent out teams to help them up and down the river. One of our men saved Pushpa's mother. She was half unconscious, clinging to a tree with one hand while with the other arm she was clasping her baby tightly to her. Her husband had disappeared before her eyes. They brought her to the *âshram* where she became a humble servant. And so that was how Pushpa happened to grow up there and unfold into a fine young girl. Everyone loved her. When she was ten years old, the Master decided she should be married. We had had with us for a year a young novice from the same district and the same caste as Pushpa. This was the man the Guru chose. It was a curious fate for that young man—he had come to the *âshram* to become a monk and now the Master was giving him a wife!

"My Guru gave Pushpa a dowry as though he had been her father and sent two monks to represent the 'bride's family' during the marriage ceremony. Beautifully adorned, Pushpa looked like a goddess. When the feast was over, she came back to live with her adopted father, according to custom in child marriages.

"From then on I was put in charge of Pushpa's education," Shrî Anirvân went on. "Until she was fifteen, her husband only came back to the *âshram* on feast days. He had found a good job in his village, took her home with him, and their married life began. Two years later Pushpa, to her delight, had a son, but the baby died in infancy. Faced with death, the young mother remained a spectator of her own grief; people heard her saying, withdrawn into herself, 'This is how it happened—the child smiled . . . and then it was all over.' 'All over' to her meant that she knew her married life was finished, for she could not have another child.

"Pushpa adored her husband with all the ardor of an eighteen-year-old. A year later, when she felt sure of her reactions, she said to her husband, 'Shankar, you must take another wife, for I do not dare raise my eyes to look at your mother so long as she has no grandson in her arms.' Before speaking to Shankar, she had made inquiries about a young girl and told him about her. Shankar said nothing, so Pushpa went ahead and arranged the marriage. Then she went away and made a long pilgrimage in the mountains. When she came back she said to the second wife, 'May there never be any bad feeling between us. Shankar is yours. You are there to serve him in everything. I chose you to give him fine children.' "

Pushpa had made her position clear. She was skillful in everything she undertook. Sometimes she would take some money from the bag in which Shankar kept his savings and would go away for a while. Where did she go? Nobody knew except Shankar.

"She used to come and visit me," said Shrî Anirvân, "and she still does. Each time she brings questions which have ripened slowly and are filled out by her experience. She listens to what I say with the intelligence of the heart that perceives what is hidden by the obscurity of the ego. You will see her tomorrow night. She has discarded so many things that she tastes life at its source. What she understands, she makes use of. And from here she will take away only what is true for her. Because of this, people are happy to be near her. Without knowing it, she transmits a living reality, but if ever she comes to realize it, the miracle will come to an end, for Great Nature will no longer work for her in the same way."

The next day Pushpa arrived with the innumerable baskets, bags, and bundles which my Hindu guests always brought with them. She was small and slender, and wore a Kashmir shawl over her shoulders. Her hair was covered by a fold of her sarî knotted round the neck in the manner of Bengali women on their way to the temple. She prostrated herself before Shrî Anirvân. As she was getting to her feet, she caught sight of me. She gripped me by the shoulders and leaned her head on my breast. Her lips were murmuring tender words I could not understand. With one hand she wiped away the tears that sprang from my eyes. I was very much older than she. All the time she was with us, she behaved to me like a loving daughter, always keeping for me the place next to Shrî Anirvân. Her awareness enriched our hours of silence. She always seemed to me contented—sorting rice or pounding spices or whatever she did. How simple life was with her!

Shrî Anirvân gave her very little time, but she did not ask for more. When she had left again with as much enthusiasm as on her arrival, Shrî Anirvân said, "Pushpa plays with time. Life has taught her that every sensation lights the flame of a little lamp in us. What matters is not to have at the same moment opposite sensations that would start a big fire. With only one sensation at a time—but that sensation has color, smell, sound—it is even tangible. This sensation has an identity! Something in us knows perfectly well where it comes from and what it is worth."

Pushpa had to spend three days and three nights on the train to get home. She traveled third class, in heat and discomfort, with an inward smile on her lips.

IX

The End of Haïmavatî

It was four years since Shrî Anirvân had sent out the call to
his pupils: "Come, everything is ready for you!" One evening
he said to me, "It is all over. The experiment at Haïmavatî
has come to an end." I did not answer. I knew it, but I
would not have been able to say when it had come about.

It is amazing to see how rapidly dissolution takes place
when nobody holds on to the fluid matters that enter into play.
I did not attempt to stop this movement of dissolution and
at the same time I was careful not to let fear enter into myself.
Fear could easily have poisoned my reactions or created sufficient lies to reassure the inner being. I wanted to keep my
eyes wide open and follow what was about to happen. I only
said, "I know it. The pupils we were expecting did not come."

"The Great Nature (*prakriti*) of India is not ripe," said

Shrî Anirvân. "Everything is too fragmentary. There is no unity yet in time. But the dream has been born and is powerful, even though lacking a body.

"What are we in the play of the great forces in action? An instrument, a means, a tool—nothing more. Let us watch this movement of dissolution taking place as it wishes; it will disappear of itself at a phenomenal speed. We are witnesses to the deviation that comes about directly after any effort. Do nothing to hinder this natural cadence. In any case you could do nothing without interference by the ego. And the ego in this case would be pure pride."

This conscious dissolution under the law was no accident; it found its own way like a phrase in music seeking another tonality. If the pupils who were supposed to have formed the nucleus of a stable team in our work had established themselves at Haïmavatî, this would have meant for me a task I had agreed to undertake for the next ten years. Influenced by their orthodox background, by the pressures of family requirements, they had not come. Nevertheless, they existed, and Shrî Anirvân was certainly going to use their energy in some other way. So far as we were concerned, the money sent from Hyderabad, Calcutta, and elsewhere had already been sent back and nothing remained but to close the house. Later, I received a letter from Shrî Anirvân, which summed up the situation as follows:

"What we created remains intact; Haïmavatî exists. It is an idea, a real idea. We had a twofold aim, that of creating a very broadly conceived Cultural Center and of preparing a retreat for those who were attracted towards spiritual research. What was lacking in our plan will come of itself, little by little, without a plan. All is *Mâyâ*,[1] which is the mystery of life."

[1] The power of illusion; the veil covering reality and the divine force producing the illusion.

The house was taken to pieces as quickly as it had been put together. Shrî Anirvân wished me to return to Europe, to take the "living idea" with me and allow it to grow freely as he himself was going to do in Assam. He foresaw that it would take me at least three years to find the right irrigated land in Europe in which to plow my furrows. To give me confidence for this new spiritual adventure, he threw a bridge out between us, as light as a spider's thread. "I shall stay here for another three years," he wrote, "but nothing will survive of what we created together except our common effort. To feel oneself 'aspirated' by the ascending law is nourishment for the whole of one's life on earth. You are going away, rich from having put your effort into an ascending law. If you are not destined to taste the fruits of this effort, it means your task is to cultivate the ground, to till it."

A few days before we left, he brought me a book which had recently appeared and which had been sent to him from Allahabad. He had read it through in one sitting.[2] "Read this carefully," he said. "It contains ideas that are very dear to us and that have been your food in these past years. Look for the people who are working in this direction; they are living for a conscious reality. You will find among them men and women who are capable of carrying an idea. This will be your first duty on arriving . . . and you keep me informed of what steps you take until you are carried by your own current."

The time of departure came near. I knew that the time lived close to a Master is a period of initiation into all the requirements of life as a whole and that the true discipline would begin for me only when I went back into the world.

"At that moment," said Shrî Anirvân, "the freedom you have acquired will give you a new sense of values in your new surroundings. Live your life leaning up against the vault

[2] This was *The Psychology of Man's Possible Evolution*, by P. D. Ouspensky (London: Hodder and Stoughton, 1951).

of the sky and with your feet well planted on the earth. Move constantly between the one and the other, remaining aware of the movements of Great Nature. It is this constant movement that is to create the matrix of the Void in which you will find yourself face to face with yourself. It is now up to you to formulate your own discipline. Above all, wipe out the past. You will be called upon to participate in different kinds of work. Enter into them and give your thoughts, your blood, your warmth, but remain free. Do not allow yourself to be eaten up by the autointoxication of your law of gravity; live with your law without going round and round in circles. Never accept any money that would bind you. Money is useful, but if you are not able to use it and remain free, then don't touch it! You know a great deal about the laws. Take what is good in them and ally it to what is good. Never go beyond what you have understood, nor what you are able to live. Principles alone are right. Do not confuse them with the interpretations that men produce. Sow seeds, water them if you are able. This is the most we can do."

I was quiet within myself when I left. At one moment when I needed reassurance, I asked, "Have I made progress in these four years that have gone by?"

"You have gone far. Before this, you were putting ideas together, crumbs of information related to knowledge. Now that is over. You are taking the time to live a totally different life." And he put a mango into my hand as he had on the day I arrived.

Shrî Anirvân left first. I took him into town as far as the bus that goes down to the plain. As we had done every day, we each folded our hands and took leave. Neither one of us spoke. We exchanged a look, very strong. When the bus had gone, it struck me that I had never touched his hand.

A week later I received the following letter:

"Today is your last day at Haïmavatî. It is also the anniversary of the day when I became a Bâül, forty-one years ago. Go forward! free and without fear, go ahead like Devahutî,[3] the mother of Kapila. May life and death be one and the same thing for you."

[3] See pp. 95f.

PART II

TALKS ON SÂMKHYA

Shrî Anirvân

Note: The teaching of Shrî Anirvân on *Sâmkhya* is given here from notes of conversations and from a number of extracts from his letters. The text has been revised by him. I asked him: "Can it be understood?" "Yes," he replied, "by one who needs it. This book is about the 'Life' of which we spoke. He who seeks the Light understands Life. It cannot be dissected without mutilating or killing it. It can only be lived, in its complexity and in its simplicity."

Narendrapur, March 1968.

I

Sahaja: Yoga in Life

Do you remember the lines I quoted from Tagore the first time you came to see me?

> Let me carry Death in Life,
> so that I may find Life in Death[1]

This is what we might call spiritual existentialism. The *Katha Upanishad* says: "The aim is to attain pure Existence (*Asti*)."[2] He who has realized it has a clear understanding of what reality is. Pure Existence is the truth beyond life and death.[3] That you exist is a fact! And your existence is nothing but a manifestation of that which is universal and transcendental. So your existence becomes oneness (*kaivalya*) in

---

[1] From *Naivedya (Offerings to the Deity)*, included in *Gîtavitâna*.
[2] Katha Upanishad 2.3.13., where *Asti=Sat*.
[3] *Rv*. X 127, 2.

which there exist the two principles of Sâmkhya[4]: *Purusha*, which is the spirit, and *prakriti*, which is "that which is manifested." Spirituality cannot be acquired; it can only be derived from these two principles.

Open yourself to the sun of pure Existence (*Sat*) as the bud of a flower opens to the light. Then the truth will flow into you. Impatience spoils everything! There is a Bâül song which says: "The stars, the suns, and the moons are never impatient. Silently, they float along the stream of pure Existence, as the true Guru does."

Now, this pure Existence, lived with a wide-open heart amid all the circumstances of life, is in itself the state of *sahaja*—a state in which the mind is freed from all duality. The motionless mind knows "that" which has neither beginning nor end, which is free in its very essence.

Sahaja is a *yoga* by the same right as all other *yogas*. It is a path that leads to the discovery of that with which one is born—the "Man," the "pure Being" seated on the throne in the temple of the heart.

In *sahaja* there is a close correspondence between the Bâül and the Sufi, provided that the "underground current"[5] of spiritual life brings the mind of both to grasp the "secret," and to live it in his own light.

As soon as one attempts to describe Hinduism in terms of circles and cycles, and Sufism in terms of four degrees, one is lost. Immediately one enters the world of division and quarrels. How is it that the Sufis have discovered the content of the *Upanishads*—that freedom of which they sing—when, in fact, the *Upanishads* are unknown to most of them? Each one, at his appointed time, must break the shell in which he is

---

[4] See pp. 92ff.
[5] This is an allusion to the sacred river, the invisible Saraswatî, which represents individual effort.

enclosed to penetrate into knowledge, just as a fully formed chick must break out of the eggshell if it wishes to live its life.

In the final stage, there is no longer any discipline, but only an uninterrupted consciousness of being. If my entire being is immersed in *sahaja* (the Sufi calls it *fana*), I "know" how, in me, without efforts, the current of a right relationship is established, which dissolves everything false or halting in my ordinary relationship with myself or with my fellow men.

The Sufis and the Bâüls tread the same path in life and drink from the same perennial source; they are above every kind of sectarianism. They do not practice any formal initiation; they speak, however, of two esoteric initiations.

One is compared to the sun touching the bud of a flower, inviting it to open. A power is transfused from the Master to his disciple simply by radiation, without ritual or words. That is all. The bud of the flower retains all its individuality.

The other initiation, of a still higher level, is compared to the sun which absorbs the dew into itself. At a glance the Master recognizes the real disciple, whether he be a Bâül or a Sufi. His look captures the reflection of the disciple's being as in a mirror; then the eyes of the Master and the eyes of the disciple close. But the current will continue to flow between them eternally. This is called the process of saturation.

But the time comes when the Master becomes the very obstacle to be overcome so that the full flowering of the disciple may take place. The cult of the personality falls away, and also the cult of ideas. The question arises, "Why do I obey?" And the answer is "the Guru of the Guru of my Guru is walking ahead on the same path as I. Can I reach the source by myself and do without any intermediaries?"

That is the beginning of a long and secret war against the Guru with many painful stages. The true Guru will be aware of this struggle. He watches closely the disorderly movements of the disciple. His kindness is such that he speaks with his disciple about "the one" who walks ahead, about the laws of inner work; but at the same time he does nothing to attenuate the struggle which has begun.

At the end of this stage is *sahaja* when the disciple finally opens the eyes of his heart and understands that he has gone astray. On this subject Keshab Das[6] has said, "I discover that I am what I was, but between the two there are nothing but complications." The aim is the truth, through which the unity of all things can be perceived. This truth is *sahaja*.

The Master of a Bâül or of a Sufi teaches nothing directly; he merely stimulates his disciple by suggestions. Once initiated, the disciple feels that a force drives him forward, but he will always have to struggle alone in the world around him, in the very heart of all life's complications.

Sahaja is a state that can be defined as follows: "That which is born in you, that which is born with you." The body, the spirit, the impulse of life, the divine intelligence—all are there. Nothing must be rejected or mutilated so that one and the same thing can be consciously established.

That is why *Sâmkhya*, which is the path to attain the state of *sahaja*, speaks a great deal of the waking state which is the normal level of all activity. It also speaks of the state of consciousness interiorized in dreams, which later becomes the state of deep sleep. The fourth state, that of inner awakening, is a witness of deep sleep. Shankarâchârya,[7] in his philosophy, gives information related to these four different states.

In *sahaja*, there is a fifth state, that of a totally awakened consciousness which contains in itself the four states of wakefulness, dream, deep sleep, and the state in which deep sleep

---

[6] In the sixteenth century.
[7] The greatest master of Monism, or *Advaita*, philosophy.

is witnessed. There is no longer any differentiation between the various states, all of them being unified at a single point.

From that moment on, everything in a flash passes before your eyes and becomes your real food. Everything is "one and the same thing in you." Then you are faced with a new task in the realm of sensation and relaxation. It becomes a question of forgetting oneself, of voluntarily obliterating the self, which is a "letting go" in a region that is very subtle and hard to discover.[8] Voluntary forgetting is a task that is just as difficult as accustoming one's mental faculty to remembering the details of self-observation. It is only approached much later, when memory has become submissive and fulfills its true role.

This is slow work—truly a discipline in itself. The effort to forget ceases when a necessary contraction for determining the field of work disappears. Without contraction there can be no direct efforts. When the effort is recognized, the contraction disappears and is immediately replaced by a very special attention—coming from very far away. This attention is at the same time indifferent to what is going on, and closely watching. It gives no orders and knows no impatience. It simply watches how Great Nature (*prakriti*) operates, for even in the subtle domain of willful forgetfulness *prakriti* has still to be reckoned with.

To forget voluntarily is, in fact, impossible for forgetting proceeds from a principle without any form. When your being is invaded by a movement coming from the heart or mind you are like a vibrating bell filled by the echo of a sound coming from nowhere.

Accept within yourself the idea that you have only twenty-four hours to live. Let these hours be resplendent with clarity for accomplishing your task. Do not allow them to be tarnished for they have been entrusted to you. These twenty-

[8] This means a forgetting of the ordinary I, that is, the superficial structure of the individual.

four hours are your eternity. In the face of this three-dimensional day, it is impossible to imagine the future. Do not attempt to stretch out time, nor to divide it, nor to lengthen or shorten it. Everything is so full, and at the same time so empty.

My one ambition has been to learn how to speak without words. That is, to be the smoke of a fire that others do not see, or the sound of music that others do not hear. It has taken me fifty years. Two ideas have always been in my mind. The first of these was to be the traveler who follows a trail with a precise goal: to touch God and to serve Him. The second was the idea of expansion: to know how to flow out like a gas without any destination, for the *Rishis* have said, "Those who have attained pure Existence (*Sat*) become the One."

Many people come to see me who only want words! If I do not speak, they are upset. So I speak in a poetic way and that keeps them occupied for a while. But where are those to whom I can entrust a task in life, one task that would be the expression of their spiritual fervor? If you are not a plowman, what do you know about plowing? If you are not a man of action, what do you know of a task to be fulfilled? In the seed of thought, action-prayer-meditation coexist in the sensation of being, and action is not what men have made of it—something subjective and hypocritical, far removed from the center of being.

You do not know that Creation itself issued from an action? To live is also an action. To live could be the action of recognizing the "Man in the temple of the heart" and serving Him perfectly.

II

Spiritual Discipline (Sâdhanâ)

When you have but once, in a flash, had a glimpse of your real individuality, why not try a discipline that leads to the expansion of the being?

The discipline of *sahaja* begins from the acceptance of the whole of life just as it is. The heart opens up to receive it and to live it. As for the intelligence and logic, they will seek in *Sâmkhya* the necessary support for finding the key to the enigma of existence. *Sahaja* then appears like a path lit by the experience of inner being.

In practice, *Sâmkhya* is the way to the realization of the expansion of *sahaja*. Neither the one, in its reasoning and logic, nor the other, in establishing the "real Man in the temple of the heart," takes into account gods, demons, paradises, hells—or formalism of any kind—in the course of inner work. The point where *Sâmkhya* and *sahaja* converge is in life, which in itself becomes the object of meditation. Therefore serenity within oneself and outside oneself a right relationship with life as a whole are the ways to an effortless *yoga*, that is, a way of being.

He who practices a spiritual discipline (*Sâdhanâ*) will use *Sâmkhya* to learn how to look at the movements of Great Nature (*prakriti*) in all its manifestations without interfering with its movements, to recognize its imprint on everything, and to observe the ability of *prakriti* to pass imperceptibly from one plane of consciousness to another. Not to react to any of its movements would mean, in fact, to live in the very heart of life without being affected by it. But at the beginning, this statement cannot be taken for granted for it is not merely by observing the movements of *prakriti* that one becomes its master.

The disciple will turn his gaze upon himself, and discover, although he had never before seen it, the countless inner disturbances created by everything in him which says: "I like and I do not like; I want and I do not want; it's right and it's wrong," and so forth, which prevent him from noticing that in himself there is a stormy *prakriti* identical to the one that exists around him.

How can he dissociate himself from that *prakriti* which until he dies will always be for him the mind and the body with all their functions? At this point traditional *râja-yoga* comes to help. This *yoga*, through its graduated disciplines, brings the body to a conscious quietness and the mind to a state of equanimity comparable to complete rest, or to ecstasy (*samâdhi*).[1] In this state of equanimity, all the automatic movements of *prakriti*, and its unconscious play can be perceived. In following this inner discipline, the ideal of *Sâmkhya* is *kaivalya*, that is to say, to learn how to stand back, and the

[1] The state of ecstasy comprising different degrees.

ideal of *yoga* is *vairagya* which means to learn how to observe oneself without passion,[2] without judgment.

Long and meticulous work is indispensable in order to discover that any emotion whatsoever creates a passionate movement which takes man out of himself. In this case *yoga* teaches how to check the impetuous movement by emptying the mind of all images. The superabundant energy is thus brought back to the self. But the purpose of *Sâmkhya* is that this energy, having returned to the self, should be directed consciously towards the outer life, that it should manifest itself openly without disturbing the inner or outer *prakriti*. In this way energy is purified. It becomes creative. Of course, this state can last only a few minutes and immediately the ordinary man reappears with his train of habitual reactions to the play of manifestation.

This moment of illumination—the word is right even if the moment be brief—is a look into oneself and at the same time a look outside oneself (*shivadrishti*). Symbolically, it can be compared to the piercing look of *Purusha* into oneself and onto the active *prakriti* around one. To accept *prakriti* in its totality is pure *sahaja*. In a subtle manner, beyond "I like and I don't like," it brings a possibility of modification in the densities of the intrinsic qualities (*gunas*)[3] of *prakriti* and shows the path by which *prakriti* can be reached.

Learn to return voluntarily to what is fundamentally primitive in you, carefully hidden and disguised in the realm of instinct, intuition, and sex. This conscious return will produce unsuspected reactions and outbursts of all your dormant impatience. If you were a tree, they would all of them be branches issuing from the same trunk. One cannot cut off one

---

[2] Which means without any emotion, emotion being closely connected with passion; see p. 202.

[3] See p. 101.

branch without damaging the whole; cutting several of them would cause the death of the tree. All branches together form the canopy of foliage.

In the wind, the foliage is in harmony with the whole forest. It is in the foliage that the birds nest and sing. May this picture help you in your spiritual discipline, even if it is very hard. If some sadness lingers in you, it means there must still be an attachment somewhere, just as in the tree there are knots which hinder the rising of the sap.

You can absorb ideas and make them your own. You can freely create ways to express them. That is what *Shakti* does, the force that is in you. Perhaps I can help you to discover your own *Shakti*—by suggestion, but nothing else. If you open up and discover who you are, I shall be pleased.

A great *tapasya* awaits you. This word means personal austerity and voluntary discipline. It is usually translated as asceticism, penance, and so on, whereas the essential Vedic meaning is nearer to the idea of radiance.

The word "*tapasya*" connects two ideas: that of heat and that of light. These are clearly the creative energy and the wisdom so often described in the *Upanishads* as together being the first manisfestation of the creative urge. One of the *Upanishads* even goes so far as to say that it is a radiation devoid of any specific characteristic, that is, without form (*alimgam*).

True *tapasya* means to be one with the creative power of *prakriti*. It brings us close to Great Nature as she really is. Through *tapasya* one drops all accumulation, all that has been acquired, and returns to what is simple and innate. The "life in the forest" of Sîtâ and Râma[4] is the perfect representation

---

[4] Râma, seventh incarnation of Vishnu, and his wife Sîtâ are the hero and heroine of the great epic poem the *Râmâyana*, attributed to Vâlmîki.

of the spirit of *tapasya*. The austerities, both mental and physical, to which many a seeker subjects himself, are only the fumbling means adopted by the ignorant soul to attain that perfectly natural end. May Sîtâ and Râma inspire you!

Allow your power to radiate and may this radiation be your *tapasya*. Hear the resonance of this call in you and have the courage to plunge unflinchingly into the depths of your soul. Do not listen to the sophistications of the wise-acres who teach with pomp and ostentation.

Rely only on yourself! An idea from the scriptures came to my mind while I was thinking of you. Do you still remember yourself when you were a girl of seventeen? When the portals of mystery were just opening before your wondering eyes? Is that girl dead? The *Tantras* say that she cannot die. Can she not be found again? Do you know her?

Understood in this manner, *tapasya* is the continuous unfolding in time of an endless intuition. There are two kinds of *tapasya*. One in which I always say "yes" (*Tantras*) and one in which I always say "no" (*Vedanta*). The true seeker who says "yes" is a born poet, for he is obliged to translate everything into exalted thoughts and language. His poetry plays the role of a science of transmutation.

III

Sâmkhya

Sâmkhya is, above all, the practical philosophy transmitted by
Kapila.[1]

Sâmkhya gives a clear idea of the *Purusha* spirit and of
prakriti represented by "Great Nature." The latter is essentially manifested in a mechanical manner, like all the cosmic
laws which govern us.

I know how difficult it is to explain deep spiritual values
to people who have been brought up in a different tradition.
That is why I think the best link between the things of the
beyond with the things of this world is that of practical
psychology. Psychology speaks a universally known language.

Sâmkhya is the only religious philosophy that speaks a
psychological language, hence a scientific language. Everything can be explained from the point of view of *Sâmkhya.*

[1] Founder of the *Sâmkhya* philosophy, who lived in the far distant
past.

It is the basis of the Buddhist *Pitakas*,[2] as well as of the Sufi precepts. It is no more concerned with rites or with dogmas than are the *Upanishads*.

Those who help to instill these broad ideas into the current of thought are doing a very important thing. In this respect, Georges Ivanovitch Gurdjieff, who followed this method stripped of any artifice, is a pioneer in the West. He is far ahead of his time; hence the virulent attacks directed against him.

Nothing exists, in any realm, that by deduction does not proceed from a higher law. There comes a time when one must submit to such a deductive process and live a spiritual existentialism. This process is pure *Sâmkhya;* it is the inexorable descent into *prakriti*, under pressure from above of the Great Will. From that moment on everything functions in a mechanical way: the higher intelligence (*buddhi*), the soul, the ego, all the centers of the human being, each one with its natural intelligence. And so it is from the moment when connections start between the different levels of the being: inner organs of perception (*indryas*), senses, constituent elements, and densities.

When "he who knows" effects the descent voluntarily, when the lowest point is reached, that is to say the nadir,[3] his "being" becomes radiant. At that moment he enters consciously into the discipline of a clearly conscious upward movement.

Man is by nature inductive; he gropes his way forward, goes blindly along. Woman, on the other hand, is by nature actively passive, for her function is to create the child. From her are born husband and father. All manifestation, mind, soul, matter, has come from her. In that respect she is the

---

[2] Teaching of the Buddha in Pàli. Collected by his disciples a hundred years after his death.
[3] See p. 96.

"Divine Mother," the foundation from which the slow ascent towards the source begins.

In *Vedanta* and for the Vedantist, if felicity is not reached in the complete passivity of all the centers, the upward path is nothing but renunciation and frustration.

The spiritual science of *Sâmkhya* can make a saint out of a man who no longer has any faith in God or in himself.

In the beginning, *Sâmkhya* appears to be appallingly dry and lacking in love, for imagination and any kind of emotion are strictly set aside. But when the inner being has recovered his lost equilibrium or discovered the equilibrium which he had thus far never felt, he is nourished by a pure love which no longer has any root in human love.

The following example, taken from Tantric *sahaja* formulates it like this: "Let your body become hard like dry wood. Then your inner felicity (*rasa*) will be like sugar syrup. Let the fire of your spiritual discipline (*sâdhanâ*) purify this syrup until it becomes candied sugar; this candied sugar will at first be brown, but finally it will become as transparent as rock crystal. May your inner felicity resemble rock crystal; then your love will be as pure as Krishna's."

In order to taste this experience, there are two means on opposite levels. In the one case, stimulants to increase sexual or other pleasures are utilized by the physical body. In the other case, the spiritual body consciously becomes more and more refined and, in full awareness, reaches a strictly graduated interiorization. This conscious lucidity will then be continuous like the tracks of a caterpillar on the earth.

A certain stage of knowledge will then be reached, that is, a knowledge that is searching for itself and gradually discovers itself. At its highest point, after a very delicate sharpening, this knowledge becomes true compassion or pure objective love.

In this attempt a Christian risks himself with difficulty, for he has to take into account a "sinful body" which weighs very heavily. The Christian places his point of support ahead of him in God, who gives him strength and consolation. He prays, invokes, and gives thanks. He is a worshiper (*bhakta*) before his Lord (*Ishtadevatâ*). The great majority of Hindus are also worshipers.

The adept of *Sâmkhya* finds his point of support in his own inner attitude, in a conscious effort to understand "what there is." To reach this attitude, he makes use of everything that he has discovered, everything that he has experienced. His material consists of events in his life which enlarge his plane of consciousness, harmonize the microcosm that he is, and reveal the relation existing between the known universe and the unknown universe around him. Although he neither prays nor petitions he has, on the other hand, an attitude of openness. He questions, he observes. He searches in himself for a familiar sensation so as to face the perfect and absolute law which unfolds. He knows that it is in meeting obstacles that the inner being will make a fresh effort to attain a wider level of consciousness. To hold to this openness entails attentive vigilance, an immense work of amassing details upon details, until the first ones are clearly perceived. To lead such a life is to live a prayer.

It is said in the *Bhâgavatam*[4] that, at the time when *Sâmkhya* arrived on the earth, a woman was the first to benefit by it. This woman was called Devahûtî. She represents *prakriti*. Devahûtî realized this knowledge to its ultimate limit, to the point of identifying herself with the "Void." She became the Void. Having rejected everything that was not the pure and luminous "I," she is said to have wandered in nature, completely naked, radiating light. At the moment of

---

[4] *Srimadbhâgavatam*, or *Bhâgavatapurâna*, is traditionally attributed to Vyâsa, author of the *Mahabhârata*.

death, instead of fading away into the Void, she transformed herself voluntarily into an inexhaustible river in order to water the whole earth and allow hundreds of thousands of beings to quench their thirst for knowledge.

As against *Vedanta*, which denies all reality, the *Sâmkhya* discipline affirms that everything is reality (*Sat*). In *prakriti*, which by nature is mechanical, three densities have to be acknowledged—matter, energy, and spirit—to reach finally the cosmic force that contains them all. Higher reality, or pure Existence (*Sat*) beyond manifestation, is expressed by the unity of these three densities. Behind it stands *Purusha*.

The essential condition of this discipline is the possibility of absorption, continually increasing until it becomes total. To start with, everything appears heavy and opaque, like a clod of earth that little by little, as understanding broadens, appears like pure rock crystal.

The soul's felicity (*vilasa vivarta*) is the state in which the unreal becomes real and vice versa.

In *Sâmkhya*, several themes for meditation are taught which date from the time of the *Vedas*.

For example, the idea of the opposite pairs of zenith-nadir (what is above and what is below), or *Purusha-prakriti*, is graphically pictured by two points linked by an ideal line going vertically from the zenith to the nadir. But in living experience one perceives in meditation that it goes on quite differently. Actually, these two poles of zenith-nadir are not opposite one another, but are joined by a continuous movement that starts from the zenith, describes a vast semicircle to the right, reaching the nadir at the bottom of the curve. After having penetrated the nadir, this same movement re-ascends to the left towards the zenith, forming the same semicircle as on the right. It gives a picture of a large round vessel with the nadir at the bottom.

The energy that descends from the zenith is fully con-

scious of its movement. In full force it condenses, breaks
down any resistance on the way, and penetrates the inner
being which, having seen it coming, has hidden itself,
coiled three and a half times, in the nadir. This coil is what
the energy has to break up.

A Guru of *Sâmkhya* explains this state as follows: energy
penetrates the dark night until it itself becomes inert, without
reaction. At that very moment it becomes entirely one with
the heavy matter.

In the nadir of *prakriti*, the threefold coil represents the
three distinct and complementary qualities (*gunas*) of *prakriti*
itself. In the descending movement, white (spirit), red (energy), and black (matter) follow one another in the order
of the colors at sunset. In the re-ascending movement towards
the zenith, the colors follow one another as at dawn: black
(matter), red (energy), and white (spirit).

The last half-coil remaining besides the three coils of the
gunas was, during the entire process of the descent, the
hiding place of the active consciousness of *Purusha*. It represents the last redoubt of the individuality-spirit through
which the re-ascent can take place.

In this picture, the conqueror, conscious of the road he
must follow, resolutely penetrates into the darkness of matter
and its heavy densities to reach the very heart of *prakriti*.
To complete his course, he has to break down the last
half-fold of *prakriti* which is holding him back. Only then
will he emerge from the struggle a hero.

Throughout the conscious and voluntary descent into the
thickness of the human being down to the nadir, a clear
vision makes it possible to perceive what will be the ascending
path starting from the nadir, for the stages and steps of the
descent are analogous to those of the re-ascent.

There is a theme of deep meditation which consists in seeing
the three *gunas* as if they were concentric surfaces, one

within the other. Thus, we have the picture of four vertical tubes which delimit them, one within the other; the one delimiting matter is outside, those delimiting energy are inside, as well as the one in the middle which delimits the spirit. The space in the center represents a zone of perfect calm, the "Void."

As soon as the perfect calmness of the inner space is perceived, the image of concentric surfaces is obliterated and the face of existing is now experienced only very subtly, as if a state of active consciousness could be compared to a thin streak of light which at the same time is filling the sky. The result is an all-encompassing sensation of fluidity along the spinal column. The sensation is that of a very fine vibrating matter ascending from below. This sensation is as the radiance of light which fills space.

The three *gunas* constitute the equilibrium of *Purusha*. Whatever takes place, the constant balance between the qualities and the substances that compose the *gunas* remains. They move always in the same order, that is, from matter (*tamas*) to energy (*rajas*), then to spirit (*sattva*), or, in the reverse order, from spirit (*sattva*) to energy (*rajas*) down to matter (*tamas*). At the time of sunrise and sunset, one can feel in oneself the very delicate transition from one density to the other, from one quality to the other, and see the change from one color to another. That is why, traditionally, these are the moments in which the *gunas* form the background and the theme of all meditation.

There are two *Sâmkhyas:* the first is philosophical, the second, mystical. Philosophical *Sâmkhya,* formulated by Ishvara Krishna,[5] is recognized in India as being the system of basic thought that indicates to the yogi, as well as to the recluse, the ascending path of spiritual search. But *Sâmkhya* is also a mystical path, enshrined in the *Vedas* and the *Upanishads,* which, in the course of centuries, has found its free and clear expression in the *Purânas* and the *Tantras,* especially in the later sacred scriptures. It can be said that the whole Tantric way of life is none other than *Sâmkhya* whose sources can be discovered in the most ancient Vedic verses.

In this, the world is not denied. The principle of supreme bliss (*Ânanda*) is recognized, but it is called by another name, *samprâsada,* which, in the *Upanishads,* is the state of "dreamless" sleep, a sleep in which the spirit is awakened within. Nothing is present to experience anything at all. There exists only a calm joy which can carry over into the waking state. There is no question of fleeing from pain, but rather of experiencing it as the embrace in which Kâlî enfolds Shiva prostrate beneath her. This is technically described in the *Tantras* by the word *viparita rati* (or the inverted coitus), in which the *Purusha* is passively accepting even death and destruction from the active *prakriti.* Evil and pain, from which the world-negating *Sâmkhya* assiduously turns away, are transformed here into bliss (*Ânanda*).

But the mystics have added something further to their

[5] The author of a treatise called *Sâmkhya Karika,* in the third century A.D. It is a profoundly negative philosophy which had an influence on the whole of life in India in the Middle Ages. This is all that is known of *Sâmkhya* in the West.

experience. They have felt that, for a realized soul, suffering
itself is no more than a ripple in the current of bliss. It
was in reference to this that Shrî Râmakrishna[6] was able to
say, "Everything is *Sat-Chit-Ânanda*. Even my suffering is
a part of the experience of being, but it has very little place
in the total experience of consciousness in bliss."

From this profound experience, *Sâmkhya*, integrated into
life as it is in the *Gîtâ*, looks upon *prakriti* as being threefold:
the lower *prakriti* (*aparâ*), the higher *prakriti* (*parâ*), and the
prakriti that is our very own (*paramâ* or *swîyâ*).

The philosophical *Sâmkhya* takes into consideration only
the lower *prakriti*, which is merely a complex of the qualities
of *sattva*, *rajas*, and *tamas*, permanently intermingled, although
one of them must necessarily predominate. But a pure quality
(*shuddha sattva*) can also exist, which is neither touched nor
soiled by *rajas* and *tamas*. This, then, would be the higher
prakriti that is many times mentioned in Puranic and Tantric
literature. This idea of pure *sattva* reigns over all the practical philosophies of the Hindu mystics.

This pure *sattva* is nothing but eternal bliss (non-existent in
rajas) and eternal illumination (non-existent in *tamas*) co-
existing in the spiritual being. This is the entire concept of
Sat-Chit-Ânanda common to the mystical philosophies of
Sâmkhya and *Vedanta*.

Vijnâna Bhikshu, a great Master of the school of *Sâmkhya* in the fifteenth century, has given us the following
metaphor in connection with *Purusha* and *prakriti*, "*Prakriti*
is *Purusha*'s wife; she is shrewd and peevish. She gives
Purusha no respite and he, completely exhausted, finally says,
'I am going away, do what you like!' Then *Prakriti* runs
after her husband in tears, implores him, and clings to him

---

[6] Shrî Râmakrishna died of cancer of the throat in 1886, at the age of
fifty, at Dakshineswar near Calcutta.

. . ." These are the two ways of dealing with *prakriti*, before and after having realized what she is. The cosmic law closest to us tells us, "As soon as you become detached from *prakriti*, it follows you."

Swâmi Rama Tirtha[7] has given us another picture, "If you turn your back to the sun, your shadow is in front of you. You can try to catch it, but you will never succeed. But the minute you turn to face the sun, your shadow is behind you. If you move, it follows you. You can make it go where you wish. The sun is truth, the shadow is *prakriti*."

It is easy for us to talk about the changes in our consciousness, the broadening of our understanding, but not so easy to speak of the readjustments of our relationship with the world, for the matter of the body is heavy. And the many envelopes of the body (*koshas*) are not illusions, as the envelopes of the mind often are.

Purusha can do nothing for us, since we are the slaves of *prakriti*. *Purusha* is outside of time and beyond our understanding, whereas *prakriti* exists in time. It is at once the aggregate of the qualities (*gunas*) that we can evaluate and the aggregate of the movements and impressions (*samskaras*) of all those qualities that make up our life. *Purusha* is a flash of perception, while *prakriti* operates in an integral mechanism.

Between the two there is the sacrifice of *Purusha*, which in time takes on a form. For example, the efforts of the Buddha can be perceived by us. If we talk about the efforts of the Buddha on our scale, we have a certain perception of something. But of what?

An exact relationship exists between *prakriti*, which moves spontaneously, mechanically, always in circles, and *Purusha*, outside of time, which merely looks on at what is happening.

[7] Rama Tirtha, who died in 1906, went to the United States after Swâmi Vivekânanda's time. While there, he spoke magnificently about *Vedanta*. He created no organization, saying, "The whole of India is my *âshram*."

In spiritual life, this relationship appears at the exact point where voluntary detachment breaks the bonds which have been established by *prakriti*. In the life of the Buddha, the period of detachment is represented by the first half of his asceticism. Later on, while looking from afar at what is happening, he becomes increasingly interested in the game in which he no longer participates and observes the smallest errors of each participant. Then, without hindering their manner of playing, he urges them by his spiritual strength alone to stand aside like himself, so that they, too, can watch the game. In this way, at the proper time, he gives them the chance to see the *prakriti* from which they are withdrawing, as he himself sees it. The subtle energy that is here described has become the aura of the Buddha; it is simply the lower *prakriti* transformed and illuminated.

In active spiritual life, one proceeds only by negation. This constant negation, for Christians, has become resignation. We must not forget that whereas in Hinduism there is no beginning, in Christianity there is no end. The way of love (*bhakti*) has its place in the attitude of negation as well as in the attitude of resignation.

The path to the attainment of the state of "divine soul" is extremely long with precipices on both sides. This state of "divine soul" is limited to a very few and, even so, is always subject to the laws of the all-powerful and mechanical *prakriti*. Jesus Christ himself was crucified; nothing was able to prevent the action set in motion by *prakriti*, which on our human level works exactly like the cosmic laws and with equal intransigence.

Prakriti contains everything that exists. It is the divine womb of all manifestation. In *prakriti* one can observe three different degrees:

1. Everything of which we are made: soul, mind, intelligence, ego, and the animal matter of our body.

2. The very principle of our possible evolution on all planes of our psychic and physical being.

3. The divine energy (*Shakti*) in its most subtle elements.

All is materiality. In the *Vedas*, the word "*tanu*" means the body as well as everything to do with incarnation, and the word "*âtman*" means the spirit and everything connected with it. These words are interchangeable and are constantly being used for one another, since they both express the same materiality. There is no difference between spirit and matter; it is only a question of different densities.

When a piece of coal is white hot, it is impossible to say whether it is burning matter or a cluster of flames symbolizing the spirit. Here we have a phenomenon of transubstantiation that is visible in the heart of the spiritual experience.

The characteristic of India is that nothing is ever rejected. What was a simple Vedic sacrifice has been transformed in the course of centuries into a ritual of such complexity that it suggests a banyan tree sheltering at one and the same time a temple, a mosque, a saint, a bandit, devotees, animals, manure, and so on. It is a real jungle in which one can easily lose one's way. In it one finds "this and that and also that."

Hence the hoarding of objects in the Hindu temples. The minute one accepts the idea of "form" (*rupa*), one can throw away nothing. Who is to decide what is true or false? Everything is of equal importance, and equally worthy of attention. Each form has a "name" (*nama*) and significance. This is so on every level.

The "too much" has a logic of its own, and logic is very far from the Divine. In the ceremonies, the forms have become all important and have driven out the spirit. With consummate art, man plays with materiality, without being aware of the mechanicalness of *prakriti*, and without discovering that he is its slave.

One cannot change the manner of being of *prakriti*, which goes its way according to a determined plan by the order of universal things, and according to immutable laws that it does not know. It knows only its own law. It does its work excellently, faultlessly. The energies divide and subdivide up to the point of feeding the cells of our body. They penetrate the heart and penetrate every drop of blood. At this point the blood is an expression of "That."

Men are tossed about and carried along by a wave, but they can swim in the direction of the cavern of the heart. There is the seat of immobile consciousness. The movement of the wave has then ceased, for men's attention resides in another order of reality. In the cavern of the heart they touch the immobile. One has to follow this process with an inward look and feel the pulsation of life. There is a known relation between the pulsation of life and the movement of the outer wave just as there is a relation between the pulsation of life and the immobile consciousness. This movement is continuous. A sudden stop would mean death.

So long as we are immersed in *prakriti*, in ourselves and in life, we are governed by it, by its movements, its whims, its cosmic rhythms. Without withdrawing into ourselves, we can have no control over *prakriti*.

It is impossible from outside to know whether the driver of a vehicle has control over himself or not. If he has, he can stop when he so decides. He knows that the wheels of the vehicle turn because of him. He is in control of his personal *prakriti*, which in its turn plays its role in a vaster *prakriti*. The latter is itself the field of action of the great cosmic laws.

There are two ways in which Great Nature constantly reacts toward *Purusha*. To remain in the center of the movement, not to be drawn to one side or the other, one must turn to the "Void," which is the beginning as it is the end of all things.

Conscious energy (*Shakti*) implies continuous growth which, even if not apparent and starting from darkness (*tamas*), is nonetheless real. It passes through the red-hot glow of active impulse (*rajas*) before reaching the whiteness of the rarefied state (*sattva*). This whiteness in life is the state of awakened consciousness.

Thus, we have to raise ourselves step by step from the plane of gross matter up to the plane of awakened consciousness, then we have to come back to heavy matter, retaining in ourselves as long as possible a continuous and right sensation. We are constantly harassed from outside by multiple shocks which call forth either the desire to see God and experience a moment of illumination or the anguish of death prowling in the shadows and bringing a state of deep depression. The dawn symbolizes the intermediate power of *Shakti*. It is the light that begins to shine in the heart of the dark night.

Perched on the shaft, the driver of the bullock cart sees the two big wooden wheels turning at the same time. One of them is life, the other death. Both wheels are equally necessary for the balance of the cart.[8]

Have the faith that shakes the world. Never say "Perhaps," but right away say "Yes." This helps you discover reactions in consciousness, to observe them and make a choice. You must not accept the slavery of automatism in your reactions. Cut it off. It is possible. Refuse categorically to be the slave of your reactions. Have a deep desire to master them.

Accept primordial nature as it exists in time, but withdraw from it and observe it from the plane of *Purusha*. The plane

[8] *Taittirîya Brâhmana.*

of *Purusha* is the plane of the spirit. This step is pure *Sâmkhya*. Believe that your evolution is possible even if your development is extremely slow.

Expect nothing whatsoever from anybody. Men are nothing but blind instruments, tools without freedom, driven by an invisible power that they do not even wish to know, for their eyes are not open. It is important to know whether our philosophy of life is effective. Only when circumstances overwhelm us do we see the movements of *prakriti* that surrounds us and notice that we ourselves are an integrated part of *prakriti*.

Then what we have perceived of pure Existence (*Sat*) nourishes our inner being, no matter what outwardly for us has taken the form of victory or defeat. It is useless to regret the past. In our life experience, we have acted according to our understanding and our possibility of that moment. This is an inescapable law which holds us in its orbit as long as we are the slaves of *prakriti*.

As soon as one consciously withdraws from *prakriti*, if only for an instant, its movement ceases. One emerges from it having touched the point of creation. This point gives an extremely pure sensation. It is often reached through "spiritual death," which is beyond all energy, beyond ramblings of the ego. But the disciple should not desire at all costs to escape from the grip of *prakriti*, for it is the field in which his own movements can be discovered, closely studied, evaluated, and used.

Every time the boatman uses the oars—they are indispensable only when going against the current—he causes a rupture in the normal flow of the river. It is the same in the flow of life. To go consciously against the current creates an opposing movement which will be manifested in one way or another.

Every movement that starts abruptly is always wrong. It

comes from an unconscious reaction in our own life, or from anguish in front of the unknown, that is, the fear of death. One must always allow the "Life principle" to run its course between an action and the decision that precedes it, and thereby allow the normal rhythm of the movements of *prakriti* to take place. The law of *prakriti* will assert its rights and create enough obstacles to strengthen or to cancel the decision before there has been any action.

It is said that thoughts that are a part of *prakriti* are of a very subtle matter. Because of that, one can learn to control them and no longer to feel one with them. When you are able to direct your thoughts in a more objective manner, it proves that you are already dissociated from them.

Every time you discover that you are dissociated from *prakriti*, even for an instant, it means that some of the elements of *prakriti* in you have been liberated. But the secret remains, that if we emerge from an impure *prakriti*, it is only to enable us to go towards a purer *prakriti*. This is the way a *sahaja* discipline lives in the heart of life. The follower of such discipline works to co-ordinate his efforts towards this end.

There are two ways of escaping the chain of *prakriti* where everything on every plane exists in such a way that experiences are endlessly repeated. Both of them are very costly.

The way of one is upward and consists either in the initiation into *sannyâsa*[9] of the monks who roam about India wearing the ocher or the white robe, or of the layman who resolutely enters, at a particular time in his life, upon the "cave life" to live a spiritual experience.

The other way tends downward. For man and woman alike, it is the degradation of prostitution, the leaving of castes, the abandoning the social framework. By this movement they

[9] Complete renunciation of worldly life by way of monastic vows.

deliberately cease to submit to one law and put themselves
under a lower set of laws.

It is not giving that counts, for giving remains a proof to
oneself that one has something to give. What counts is to
taste the most complete dissatisfaction with oneself and to
see it with open eyes until one gets down to bedrock. This
is the movement that causes *prakriti*, uncovered and un-
masked, to react. At this moment something as yet unper-
ceived can begin to break through. It is the energy (*Shakti*)
that becomes the matrix, or the "Void." Then something can
take shape and be born when the time comes. Bedrock represents the eternal *prakriti* busy with ceaseless creation, for
such is her function, indifferent to everything taking place
around her. This is one of her movements. She has another
one, opposed to the first, which must also be discovered.
According to one of her laws, she gradually pushes her children into *Purusha*'s field of vision. Meeting the piercing look
of *Purusha*, whose function it is to "see," is an instant of total
understanding, a giving up of oneself. How can one describe
that look? What one knows of it cannot be communicated.
And besides, it would be useless to try.

All one can do is to wait with much love and be ready
to meet it. Is it possible to guess when *prakriti* will make a
sign to you? Is it possible to know why she does so?

It is essential to build one's life around two principles:
that of contraction and that of expansion. The moment of
complete, conscious "letting go" is when *Purusha* is in dissociation from *prakriti*. Such a moment lasts no longer
than the time it takes to breathe in and out a few times; this
creates the naked universe, stripped of the "I." Correctly
speaking, this is not meditation, but rather an attitude of interiorized life. Shrî Aurobindo lived it for forty years, isolated

in his *âshram*[10]; Shrî Râmana Maharshi lived it during his whole life.

Expansion is the creative moment corresponding to introspection. The one inevitably leads to the other, that is, expansion of itself leads to "letting go" when one finds the inner point of balance.

An all-embracing idea is that of conscious identification with the forces of nature. Its significance is vast. It means full expansion in the being. But one cannot actualize anything without first having let go of everything!

What can I do? Faced with this question, the best thing to do is to do nothing out of one's own initiative, but simply to watch how things are being done. What we call "our" will is not really ours. It is simply an upsurge of the vast *prakriti*. Patience! If the bud has come, the full bloom is sure to follow. Then why be in haste? All creations are noiseless. Unfold yourself, or, rather, let *prakriti* unfold herself in you. Your only duty is to retire and at the same time to be alert.

The idea of expansion has to be properly understood. There can be no expansion except through love. In love we come out of our little ego. But this love has to be impersonal. I can speak to you about it by using the Vedic image of the sun, which radiates energy and thereby illuminates, loves, and creates. This is the essence of its expansion. It is not attached to anything, yet it attracts everything to it in its kingdom of light. Expansion does not mean doing something; it means being and becoming. The capacity to do flows spontaneously from the capacity to be.

Purusha "is," whereas *prakriti* can only "do," and always from the center outwards, exactly the way the very delicate green shoot sprouts from the germinated seed. This seed in

[10] Shrî Aurobindo appeared only four times a year before his disciples, on the days known as *darshan*.

itself is *Purusha* folded back on itself, motionless and at the same time the creator of the movement of life. You must know this, and then feel that in yourself you are both *Purusha* and *prakriti*. This is the *Sâmkhya* version of expansion.

I often wonder who orchestrates the dangerous games of nations, who it is that in a given year devours the sap of life, and in another year gives it fresh vigor. All this is the work of *prakriti*. How clever she is to create mountains out of a grain of sand! From afar *Purusha* watches her at work. He smiles! To tell the truth, *prakriti* also laughs while pretending to be absorbed in the work on which her heart is set!

The important thing in all this is to keep calm and smile at it all while taking everything as it comes up just as seriously as would a child. Then forget it the next minute! There will always be heavy obligations to carry, but you can lay them down, one after the other, as you move forward on the road of life.

These obligations are like black clouds accumulating in the sky. When they become heavy enough, they burst of themselves and disperse. In time, obligations disappear by themselves.

The secret is to accept everything, but be very careful not to be attached to anything whatsoever!

IV

Laws—Powers

In India people strive for these powers:

- —to reach God;

- —to make God objective;

- —to have a clear sensation of the "I";

- —to eradicate every difference between "you" and "me";

- —to materialize the divine laws and worship them as
  they are represented in the forms of gods.

If man of 50,000 years ago were to return, he would see
that man has not changed—neither spiritually nor in his deep
reactions. The whole of civilization is only the outward appearance of what is manifested (*Mâyâ*). So why then would

the Hindu devotee not look for a means to escape from this slavery?

This cosmos to which we belong does not hold us in slavery. It is what it is. For us it represents the continuity of a power, of a descending law with, here and there, one ascending soul—one in a million, says the *Bhagavad Gîtâ*.

Such a soul radiates its own light; it touches other hearts because it has "passed through the death of the ego to the birth of the being." It is nourished by the Void. In the Void, absurdities evaporate spontaneously.

He who has lost faith and builds it up again, slowly and cautiously, by means of the science of *Sâmkhya*, the logic and mathematics relating to cosmic laws, knows by experience why the world holds together; but the instant he tries to formulate the mathematical equation, he will fall again.

Râma, the seventh incarnation of Vishnu, is still venerated in India today as he has been for several thousands of years. Not only is he the perfect hero of the *Râmayâna*, but he also represents, as symbolized by his green face, Great Nature in her eternal recurrence, a form of *prakriti* that the human heart can comprehend. That is why the name of Râma is chanted in the litanies as the dead are borne to the cremation ground.

The life of Râma during his exile in the forest, his veneration for the holy hermits, are a delight to millions of Hindus in their old age. His wife Sîtâ, born of the earth, sprang up from a furrow when her father, King Janaka, was plowing and symbolizes the impulse of *prakriti* towards *Purusha*. Râma and Sîtâ express two opposite movements of power, the one ascending, the other descending. Their role is to bring mankind and organic life on earth into the play of cosmic laws. Hence the importance of those wonderful litanies called *Sîtâ-Râm* which are sung on the days of *Ekadashî*. These special days are the eleventh day of the waxing and of the waning of the moon. Fasting is a rule. This is such a firm habit that everyone fasts without ever mentioning it.

Shrî Râmakrishna's gift of mime—he had been an actor in his youth—came out in his ability to give a concrete form to the sacred lives of the gods. He played consciously with the laws represented by the gods. Submitting to the laws, he at the same time knew how to use them.

Shrî Râmakrishna showed the mechanical aspect of the laws. Man, according to his stage of evolution and inner attitude, sees in them miracles, ironies, or absurdities in order to escape the grip of eternal recurrence. At the same time, he refuses to see the operation of these cosmic laws. This operation is beyond human logic, human logic being only a form of the unconscious and mechanical functioning of the ego.

A little *sâdhu* lived according to the law of the bee making its honey (*mâdhukari*). According to this law, he had the right to go every morning to the door of three houses and ask for food, but without uttering a word. If he received nothing, there was nothing to do but fast.

One day all he received were two *chapatis* (wheat cakes). While he was eating them, the tears flowed down his cheeks, for his hunger was not appeased. He did not complain, but said to God, "What dost Thou wish me to do on two *chapatis?*" Before the words were out of his mouth, a passer-by stopped him and said, "We have come here to have a picnic under the trees. Do us the honor of being our guest for the day. Please come and eat with us."

The world is a bazaar where everybody is shouting at the top of his voice to attract attention and make his little bargain. Remember that outward success or failure means nothing. All is the play of the divine. All depends only on how the game is played. Thoughts are a thousand times deeper than words.

Be deep, be steady, be dumb in the agitation around you. Let the powers act without allowing a little human law, subjective and narrow, to interfere. The great powers act by impregnating the nerve fibers of the earth.

The whole of life is the immensity of night (*varuna*) and the immensity of light (*mitra*). The multiplicity of the circumstances and conditioning, to which we are subject in time, must not distort our inner vision in relation to darkness and light.

Then, in the intermediate light between day and night, we will clearly distinguish the broken lines which are the laws as they come down to us and insofar as we are able to understand them. The work, for every one of us, is to learn to recognize them steadfastly and patiently one after another.

Power, even in its most subtle and essential vibrations, already includes two directions: one is positive and the other negative. Words such as "truth," "life," "essence" should only be used with caution, for they contain an implicit source of opposition.

All the *Rishis* have repeatedly taught that spiritual life goes by leaps and bounds, by thrusts whose trajectory, being subject to the law of gravity, falls down again from the apogee of its course. This fall creates eternal recurrence. We live and are fed by the visions of "those who see," and there will always be new *Rishis* and new disciples.

In fact, the *Rishis'* vision serves only to create disciples. Disciples are necessary so that what is brought by the *Rishi* can make its way into life. The more the disciples are attached among themselves, the more mediocre they become, interested only in their rights of seniority, their *âshram*, their brotherhood, their Master's thought, without themselves being engaged in the process of creation.

The *Rishi*'s vision does not seem to belong to those who gather around him, but is testimony to "That which is" for a much wider circle and for the sake of a continuity that will take care of itself. This vision is a state of impersonal consciousness; it is what keeps the world in an exact relationship to the laws. To impose a name on it is to limit the vision and lock it in a closed circle.

There are three important points to recognize in the ascending spiral representing the evolution of man: the point of sunrise, the point of the zenith, and the point of the "high north," or *uttaram*, which is the summit reached by trajectory of the ascending spiral. The "high north" is the point where a new light scale begins to develop.

This direction towards the "high north" is also directly related to the solstices. The sun travels towards the north from December 21 until June 21 and the days lengthen. From the time when the sun moves towards the south, the days get shorter. This is why Yama, the king of Death, is represented as living in the south and Shiva, the god of Life, in the north. The east is the origin of light, the west is the house of the "Void." These indications are scrupulously observed in the building of a temple or of a house. The position northeast always indicates the very action of the law.

For an action to be in accordance with the laws and be a part of them, the two poles must support it. One of them is the Void, which generated the action, the other the energy and freedom of its movement.

Such a movement is established in a right relationship between Guru and disciple. The Guru says to his disciple, "Go and fulfill this task and know that I am here. I shall be the Void of your movement. Feel this deeply in yourself." These two poles can also co-exist in the same person, which is the state mentioned in the *Bhagavad Gîtâ*: the action born from the vibration of the Void.

The best illustration of this is the story of a nun chosen by the king of a state to become his queen. The *sannyasinî* finally accepted on condition that she be given a private room in the royal palace to which she alone would have the key. She used to go there every day. The king, jealous of the radiance of the queen, decided one day to follow her there to steal her secret. The room he saw her enter was bare and whitewashed. A sackcloth robe was hanging on a nail. The queen took off her rich attire and her jewels and put on this beggar's dress. Then she meditated for a long time, seated on the ground. At last, she turned around and said to the king, "Here I am 'myself,' the woman who loved God alone before she became a queen, and who still loves only God, in His divine play."

That queen has no name. She is part of Indian folklore.

An impulse pushes us to follow the way of the spirit (*Purusha*). We must not stop to ask: "What is this impulse?" It is there so that we may follow it and make it grow. No backward steps! This impulse has to be cultivated because it belongs to the ascending law.

On the other hand, *prakriti* holds us fast in the wheels of her perfect machinery. One can be satisfied there and sleep in peace. *Prakriti* asks no more of us. She has a very strong power of gravitation, and drags back to her beings who were ready to escape. She brings them back very skillfully for she needs our lives for her own purposes; she needs humus composed of constantly renewed and subtle matters which our lives bring to her.

About your personal discipline, you are following the right course. What you get through intuition can never fail you. The whole attitude can be summed up in a short sentence: "I know it, I feel it, I am it." Let the powers work deep within you. The pain that results is that of a new birth. If inclination for inner work lessens, do not worry. Creation starts in darkness. Out of nothing, *Shakti* comes. Let yourself flow with the stream; do not struggle. Not that you will reach the shore; your destination is to become the ocean itself.

We know that there are seven planes: three above and three below and a seventh which serves as a bridge. The three lower planes generate the physical, vital, and mental; the three higher generate pure Existence (*Sat*), pure radiant Energy (*Chit*), and Bliss which is the joy of creation (*Ânanda*); the seventh plane is that on which things are carried out, that of the mother standing between the father and the child.

In *Tantra* the lunar days are divided into three groups of five. This fivefold pattern symbolizes the power of the Virgin-mother. In each group, the days stand for joy (*nandâ*), harmony and welfare (*bhadrâ*), victory and might (*jayâ*), consecration and Void (*riktā*), fullness (*purnâ*). *Shakti* is pictured as a little girl growing into womanhood. The first stage is her childhood; the second, her adolescence; the third, her maturity. The following two are beyond growth, they are the eternity of the Void and the fullness. The same applies to the three lower planes: physical, emotional, mental. Beyond *Shakti* is the eternal spirit known as *Shodashî*, and beyond it complete emptiness, *Nirvânakalâ*.

The full moon symbolizes the blossoming of the new moon (creative activity working in darkness). This is why peasants who are in contact with the earth sow for flowers during the bright half of the moon and for fruit and grain in the dark half. The dark ray of creation is spoken of in the *Katha Upanishad*.[1]

Following is the scheme of the seven planes:

Father	Mother (the bridge)	Child
1, 2, 3	4	5, 6, 7

[1] 2.2.15.

There is always a gap, a no man's land, between two planes. Otherwise there could be no creation. The Buddhists were right in saying that "Everything" comes from "Nothing."

The intrinsic qualities (*gunas*) of *prakriti* are what bring different degrees of modification in the movement from matter to spirit and vice versa. These modifications are everywhere and on all planes. As I have told you, energy (*rajas*) is the element of fermentation. The *Bhâgavatam*[2] gives a beautiful comparison between the entire process and a piece of wood catching fire. At first there is no fire—a state of inertia (*tamas*); then comes smoke—a state of energy (*rajas*); and then heat and light—the rarefied state (*sattva*). So whenever we try to break up inertia on the human plane, we must be ready for "smoke" (confusion, misunderstanding, rashness); these things are bound to happen. The whole world is *rajas*, storm and stress, otherwise matter could not become "luminous spirit," or the "multiple in harmony" like the petals of the lotus which is the symbol of the One.

Dissolution is often necessary before real creation starts. You cannot be always looking for something. You must stop somewhere and let things grow within you. There is a rhythm of creation and a rhythm of dissolution, symbolized by the dance of Shiva. At first, this dance is violent, full of convulsive movements with steps marking life and death at the same time. The *Rishis* have called this part of the dance *Tândava*. Its duration is related to cycles. Gradually the dance changes into the soft dance of *Shakti* where the rhythm becomes supple, life and death near each other, felt in the same movement. The *Rishis* have called this rhythmic vibration *Lâsya*.

Herein lies the true creative possibility of *Shakti*, of which the violent *Tândava* of Shiva is the cosmic background. The balance and deep significance of life lie in dissolution. This is what makes life a constant renewal. Accept things just as they come and one day the light *Lâsya* step will be yours.

There are two movements in creation. The interiorization always precedes the exteriorization. It is represented in the following imagery: according to the *Purânas*, creation was to come from the conjunction of four united principles, the four sons of Brahmâ.[3] But when Brahmâ had created them, instead of going down to earth and manifesting themselves outwardly, they went back into their father's bosom and became the force of resistance (*Shakti*) from which there then issued the "Seven Sages" or "Seven laws" which participated in the creation and continue to maintain it. These two movements, interiorization and exteriorization, are to be found everywhere, in creation as in de-creation, or *pralaya*, that is to say, the creation that undoes itself spontaneously beginning from the end. Creation is in itself birth and death, whereas de-creation is in itself death and birth.

Shrî Râmakrishna perceived these two movements very clearly. He gave his wife, Sâradâ Devî, the Tantric power of expansion by which she created conscious men around her who called her the Holy Mother. On the other hand, Shrî Râmakrishna gave to those young people who were attached to him the concept of interiorization of *pralaya*, like that of the monk "sucking in" the universe, or the bird coming down from the sky without ever touching the earth.

It is difficult to conceive the transition from rarefaction to density even though it is the process itself of all creation. We realize, or rather we imagine, what the Void may be, but to follow the process of the ether becoming the earth, which is the genuine realization of creation, is an extremely arduous task.

[3] The god of the Hindu trinity in his creative aspect.

You rise to the heights and are often aware of the process, but then you suddenly bump on the earth. Of course, you bring the aroma of the ether into the earth but still you cannot divinely create it. The task has been given up as almost impossible by the author of the *Brahmasûtra* who remarked, "You can become one with Brahmâ in knowledge and bliss, but you cannot become one with Ishvara in his creative power." The thing is something like this: you can die at your will, but you cannot be born that way. If you could do so, your birth would be a divine birth—an incarnation.

For ages man through idolatry pursued his quest beyond death. Even nowadays man's search starts with idolatry, and a very important thing to see is that it ends with it, too. If matter becomes spirit, spirit, too, must return to matter. That is why the greatest spiritual masters of India never denounced or gave up idolatry. Not even Shankarâcharya.

In his Guru's teaching, the Hindu disciple discovers, in the spiritual discipline he follows, how to put into daily practice the laws of Shiva Mahâdeva, the supreme Lord, just as they are described in all the sacred texts. These laws are illustrated by three aspects of life—creation, preservation, and destruction—and by two movements—the one from above going downwards, the other from below going upwards.

The disciple will hold to this imagery so long as he expects to receive everything from his Guru. He may continue to do so during several successive lives, unless the idea of evolution is born in him. There comes a time when the disciple recognizes the obstacles that he must face and go beyond. He discovers that this has to do with the Law of Three in his own nature and development.

Three laws govern life: the law of growth, the law of expansion, and the law of intensity. All three are illustrated by the "Tree of Life," showing how the tree grows, how it spreads out its foliage, and how it sinks its roots deep into the soil.

You must be firmly rooted. Such is the first law. Then grow and assert yourself. At this moment open yourself, stretch out your arms to feel your radiation around you, and then bring the universe back to you with your head held high, for it touches the sun. Be deep, wide, tall, truly a Tree of Life.

Shakti, insofar as it is the principle of matter utilized by *Purusha* in its manifestation, still depends on *Purusha*. It is by nature opposed to *Purusha*, so that between the two a life-bringing current may be established. As soon as *Shakti* appears, it already contains in itself the three initial laws which give it its material density.

If *Purusha* chooses to play an active role, its *Shakti* will always be passive. On the other hand, if *Purusha* chooses to be passive, its *Shakti* will always be active. While the passive element stands back, the active element takes different forms. Each form, each movement gives rise to new laws which, if the movement ceases, will be reinfolded in one another and return to the initial force which gave them birth.

Thus, in Shivaism, Shiva, representing the spirit, is always passive, and his *Shaktis*, representing various aspects of manifestation in the world, have different functions under different names: Uma, Gaurî, Annapurna, Parvatî, Kâli, Durga, and so forth. In Vaishnavism, on the other hand, Vishnu is the active element. He is the creator who has manifested himself in different forms in different incarnations,[4] displaying a gradual voluntary evolution. The constant activity of Vishnu is to maintain the world, whereas his *Shakti* is secret, inner, com-

---

[4] There are ten incarnations of Vishnu (*Bhâgavatapurâna*, Bk. I, Chap. 3).

pletely passive. She is called Shrî, meaning beauty, harmony. She is the symbol of the lotus in full bloom. Shrî is the secret in the heart of woman. Beside Râma she is Sîtâ; beside Krishna she is Râdha.

The sound (*bîja*)[5] in the sacred word (*mantra*) is the vibration which causes matter to pass to spirit, or inversely spirit to pass to matter. Hence its great importance in spiritual techniques. Every being has his own vibration which, either clear or confused, is equivalent to a formula of a possible coagulation or dissolution. On the horizontal plane, in ordinary life, this mantric vibration is expressed by a surface (*yantra*) which is the basic individual diagram used by the force emanating from the self at whatever degree of materialization.

This force flows out in complete disorder. It is instinctive. It obeys all the outer attractions and associates with all the automatic movements of *prakriti*, whatever they may be. Those who are conscious of the power of this spontaneous force direct their effort towards stopping its uncontrolled emanation, to canalize it without provoking any mutilation.

Then one must learn to know it, to direct it, to love it as it is so as to tame it and give it a way of expression. The sacred sound (*bîjâ*) is that very force which, when necessary, is used against itself. This has nothing to do with the repetition of invocations or sacred words (*mantras*) which are used to create a state of openness or surrender; but only with the syllable which is the seed.

There are four Tantric laws which concern Unity:

1. Cosmic unity (*brahmânda*), which is in the expansion of the self up to touching the sky, a passionate love for the sensory universe in all its forms, until it brings in oneself

[5] This sound is the very seed sown by the Guru. See p. 144.

the vibration of the words: "The Earth is my mother, I am the child of the Earth."

2. The psychic unity (*prakrityanda*) existing between the real inner being and the ego with all its impulses. This unity is the thread of life connecting all experiences until the discovery of knowledge.

3. Causal unity (*mâyânda*), which is the progressive discovery of the forces and laws of *prakriti*.

4. Spiritual unity (*shaktyanda*), which is the harmonious association of our soul, our essence, the "I," with the force of life—the most subtle *prakriti*.[6]

There is a basic rule for approaching any of these laws, which is to understand that the body is the instrument of life. It follows that any stiffening or hardening, that is, any tension in thought or in the body, prevents a conscious extension towards the infinite.

Now, as regards the spiritual quest. If you consciously hold within yourself three quarters of your power and use only one quarter to respond to any communication coming from others, you can stop the automatic, immediate, and thoughtless movement outwards, which leaves you with a feeling of emptiness, of having been consumed by life. This stopping of the movement outwards is not self-defense, but rather an effort to have the response come from within, from the deepest part of one's being. This process reverses the natural movement of *prakriti* and brings back energy to its seed form. Let this become your way of communicating with others.

Something in yourself is awakened, and by this interiorization you set in motion a movement in the direction opposite from what is taking place outwardly. Thereby two movements are created in you. One of them goes outward and the

---

[6] In the *rândakyopanishad*, these unities have been represented by four levels of *brahmavija*—consciousness, corresponding psychically to the four stages of consciousness described on p. 84.

other goes inward. The latter is the movement of the higher *prakriti* uniting with the immobile *Purusha*. This is the moment in which *prakriti* surrenders, in which there is no struggle.

The law of life is the same. As the physical cells build the body, the germ cells are concentrated within and retain their energy for a later creation. We imagine that we create by projecting outwards, whereas real creation takes place through suction and absorption. When this power of absorption becomes natural, you discover that creation, radiation, communication and all similar processes come to you spontaneously.

In *Sâmkhya*, this spontaneous creation is called *Dharma-Megha*, or the cloud of energy that pours forth multiple powers, for behind this creation there is the Void.

All spiritual search is directed towards a shining point, which can be approached only from the periphery of a big circle and in many different ways. *Sâmkhya* is the logical science that makes it possible to see the movements of *prakriti* and to dissociate oneself from it on the plane of life itself. This is the opposite of the attitude of so many seekers who, to escape from the clutches of *prakriti* and turn away from it, run away from the world and practice a primitive discipline that mutilates their life to the point where it no longer has any connection with reality.

Feeling oneself dissociated from *prakriti* does not mean that one has become her master. To master *prakriti* requires inner work and attentive observation of *Shakti*'s energy. This energy is power fully awakened, but not tamed. Only when *prakriti* is conquered and mastered does Life within life, life in the midst of all *prakriti*'s erratic movements, become the state described as Shiva-*Shakti* in the heart of the cosmic laws.

The whole theory of the Void is that of that luminous ether (*âkâsha*). Sound (*vak*) and speech come from *âkâsha*, hence the idea of a creative God who, to manifest Himself, uses five elements and five sensations.

The five elements belong to God, to the descending law; the five sensations belong to man, to the ascending law. To come to direct experience, the only authority we have is the Sacred Scriptures and the experiences of the saints and yogis who have gone before us. The work of transformation in the course of evolution can only be done by oneself on oneself. A Master, of course, can activate it, fellow disciples can help in sustaining the effort, but the seeker will be entirely alone thoughout his attempt and many times he will confuse the means with the end to be attained.

Some notions are occasionally given but always in a veiled form which can be interpreted in different ways, such as:

"One must be subtle enough to feel the presence of the mother, for life begins with an odor . . .
"One must be subtle enough to discover where the father is, for life ends with a sound . . ."

In studying the *Tantras*, one discovers progressively, thanks to sound and by means of sound, how the idea, by taking on density, gradually becomes the object that is perceived. The two-words "Shiva-*Shakti*" in conjunction create the vibration by which the spirit takes on the density of matter. Every time this double word is pronounced one must refer to what it contains in the ascending law, for it is the passage from one stage to the other. In every sensation pertaining to the ascending law, each movement begins with heat, continues with the materiality of food and light, and reaches luminous ether, that is, the Void.

The three laws of *Shakti* always remain veiled. They are the laws of pure Existence (*Sat*), of pure Spirit (*Chit*) and pure Bliss (*Ânanda*). Another law, however, the law of phenomena, is projected onto the screen of consciousness.

The first of the three laws is that of pure Existence. *Sat*, although it has the appearance of complete immobility, is in itself a vibration, a movement. This inner vibration is the source of all existing movement. The first movement is a straight line between two points and it is this straight line that represents the immobility of Shiva. *Prakriti* appears and takes possession of the pattern of straight lines, weaving on it her pattern in the shape of a spider's web, with broken lines tangential to concentric circles.

Lastly, by the force of *Shakti* these tangential broken lines detach themselves from the horizontal plane to form a spiral around its axis.

The second law is the law of pure Bliss. *Ânanda* is the result of the movement having taken place in consciousness, a calm movement like an undulation of the water. These undulations contain life, which is in itself the very essence of *Shakti*. This pattern of soft undulation is nevertheless made up of short broken lines.

The third law is the law of pure Spirit. *Chit* has a very definite function between the vibration originating in the immobile point and the wave that is the essence of *Shakti*. It is the awakened consciousness and its role is to unite *Sat* with *Ânanda.*

In one way or another, it can be said of *Sat* that if I look within myself, I see that *Shakti* attracts me inwardly. I become conscious of the immobility of the world and of the straight line between two points representing *Purusha.* Of *Ânanda* it can be said that if I am conscious of what is around me, I project myself outwards and enter into the very play of *Shakti.* At this moment I feel all the waves passing over the water as being the pulsations of life itself. On the other hand, *Chit,* pure consciousness of the spirit, observes what is happening between *Sat* and *Ânanda.*

The expression Shiva-*Shakti* reveals the ultimate reality beyond the concept *Purusha-prakriti* of classical *Sâmkhya.* Shiva-*Shakti* is the state of the fully realized being, that is, an inward state of enlightened consciousness. The seeker who has not yet dissociated himself from the *prakriti* outside himself and from the *prakriti* within himself, sees the immobile *Purusha* as a state of pure consciousness and *prakriti* as being an unconscious and mechanical force.

Prakriti and *Shakti* thus denote two different states of consciousness, the second being a higher state of consciousness tending towards the "limitless." *Prakriti* is a kinetic energy, whereas *Shakti* is a latent potential energy returning to itself and containing in itself all the possibilities of development of *prakriti*'s movements.

If I speak to you, I am using *prakriti*'s power of exteriorization. If I collect in myself what I wish to say to you, I have the choice of speaking if I so desire or of saying nothing, thus demonstrating the interiorized power of *Shakti* which contains in itself the kinetic capacity of *prakriti.*

The inner fluctuations and commotions in the course of

spiritual discipline (*sâdhanâ*) can be expressed schematically, showing the modifications in the passive and active qualities at work.

The lower aspect of exteriorization	*prakriti–Purusha*	
	+	−
The higher aspect of interiorization	Shiva–*Shakti*	
	−	+

From the point of view of *Sâmkhya*, *prakriti* can be an active energy only if it has a passive substratum opposing its movement. This is represented mythologically by Kâlî (time) dancing on the naked body of Shiva (the Infinite Space). From the psychological viewpoint, consciousness is the surface of a mirror across which reflections of the movement pass rapidly. Consciousness remains immobile.

In the mystical experience a question arises: *prakriti* in movement and immobile *Purusha* are but one. Here the *Vaishnavite Tantras* bring a clarifying element to *Sâmkhya* by saying that the visible movement in *prakriti* is *Purusha*'s movement permeating it. The two are no longer dissociated. Spiritualized *prakriti* is nothing more than the form of *Purusha*. Mystically, this gives us the following diagram:

Prakriti–Purusha	the two movements of existence having become one.
Krishna–Râdha	the mystical couple par excellence.

Krishna, as *Purusha*, is fully conscious in the midst of his activity. Râdha, in her transcendental love for Krishna, is in ecstasy (*samâdhi*) even in her role of *prakriti*. Psychologically, according to *Vaishnavite* Tantrism, Râdha, through her passivity, becomes the substratum of the activity of Krishna-*Purusha*. The roles are thus reversed, producing the following diagram:

Shiva—   Kâlî+
passive consciousness   active *prakriti*

Krishna+   Râdha—
active *Purusha*   effacement in love

Shiva—Râdha are *nirguna*   the transcendental aspect of existence and power

Kâlî—Krishna are *saguna*   the phenomenal aspect of existence and power.

That is why, in India, so many children are named Kâlî-krishna.

In *In Search of the Miraculous*[7] many points have a link with the Tantric scriptures which reveal the necessary deviations making it possible for creation to escape from the ceaseless mechanical repetitions of *prakriti*.

If there were no deviation, one could easily imagine creation taking place without discontinuity between the immoble *Purusha* and *prakriti* manifested in its numerous aspects. But the primordial energy of *Shakti* constantly produces deviations, both in the subtle densities of the spirit and also in the coarse densities of matter. Once set in motion, this process cannot stop. Therein lies the whole chance for creation towards a possible evolution, and man's opportunity to move upwards, provided that the deviation by broken lines turns upward in a spiral. The amplitude of the curve can be very wide without change of direction.

The curve of deviation can also move away, or be repeatedly retraced on the horizontal plane, attracted by its point of departure. In that case, because of the endless rep-

[7] P. D. Ouspensky, *In Search of the Miraculous: Fragments of an Unknown Teaching* (New York: Harcourt, Brace and Co., 1949).

etitions, the primordial energy is frittered away and finally will be lost.

The figure "3" represents the "Law of Three," which contains the whole of life. In the beginning, there was the One, *Purusha*. From its inner vibration, the One projected its opposite, as light casts a shadow, which is its substratum. In this movement, spirit-matter can be perceived, bound by the energy which belongs equally to the one and the other. This can be demonstrated in the following manner:

One is the I-subject manifested by light—*sattva*
Two is the I-object manifested by shadow—*tamas*

Between the two aspects of I-subject and I-object the everlasting movement of life develops, that is, all forms of manifestation on the lower plane of life. This everlasting movement of energy is *rajas*.

Thus life, through the energy of *rajas*, is a development of movements acting between the two poles of *sattva-tamas*. From the plane of *rajas*, which is ours, a certain state of consciousness can exist in which it is possible to perceive what is above (*sattva*) and what is below (*tamas*).

What is above can be known by sudden intuition or glimpsed through imagination, but one cannot actually reach it without a shock provoked by the vision itself. A thorough discipline of the mind is the indispensable preparation for this.

What is below is the weight of ignorance, the inertia of the primitive *prakriti*. It is also the field of individual work. Before discovering the stages leading towards *sattva*, one must become conscious of the descent towards *tamas* and become familiar with the opposition of heavy matter.

The energy of *rajas* proceeds from *Shakti*, which holds sway in the space between *sattva* and *tamas*. The energy of *rajas* is the desire that creates life. Without this desire, that space would be the Void without movement or action. Actually, life exists only through a deviation of energy, through a propulsion which sooner or later returns to its starting point.

This movement of exteriorization and of interiorization seems to vary in its possibility of extension according to one's understanding of it. In fact, one stands in front of a point • (*bindu*) which contains everything in itself. When energy creates a movement, this point becomes a straight line. To return to its starting point, a deviation is a necessity. The straight line will break and, through broken lines forming angles, will return to its starting point.

Three angles are necessary to enclose a space and thereby by this movement create a surface, a form. This form is a triangle. Every action can be described as a triangle. If the angles are equal, the action is perfect and balanced. The three lines are the qualities of *prakriti* (*gunas*) and the space is that of *Shakti* spread out and in balance. *Shakti* can also gather itself together at the central point (*bindu*) which signifies—in a perfect action or in a perfect meditative state— the union of *Shakti* and *Purusha*, a state of perfect awakened consciousness.

But life is full of distorted and falsified actions, that is, of triangles with unequal angles in which the central point has been displaced in relation to the center of the perfect triangle. The cause of the deviation is unconscious subjectivity, the desires and greediness of the individual *prakriti*. Innumerable triangles can be formed on the base (*tamas*) of the triangle, which are projected up to the line of consciousness. This line is not continuous; it is made up of an infinity of points that represent short moments of consciousness.

The following diagrams serve as illustrations:

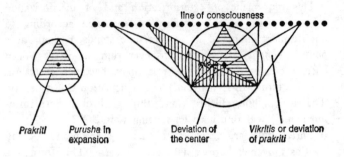

Prakriti   Purusha in   Deviation of   Vikritis or deviation
             expansion   the center   of prakriti

At a certain time while following a spiritual discipline a man tries by interiorization during active meditation to feel in himself the mobile qualities and tendencies of the inner being. It means to come into contact with the world in which his own Law of Three functions. On our level of understanding we can perceive the triangle of our life formed by the three *gunas* and the numerous irregular triangles formed by our actions.

The subdivisions are an expansion of the three *gunas* (*tamas-rajas-sattva*) in relation to the three fundamental intrinsic qualities of the primordial *prakriti*. These divisions make up different worlds in accordance with their relative distance, the one from the other. The more the subdivision of the *gunas* increases, the greater is the subdivision of the Law of Three. A seeker can never have access to any world higher than his own unless he has completely absorbed in himself the *gunas* of his own world to the point of being one with them. This means that his inner balance is then brought into accord with his *prakriti*.

In the following diagrams, the figures indicate the number

of *gunas* in each world. From one world to the next, the number is multiplied by two, whether the worlds are taken as in the cosmic order or as worlds interiorized in man. The number represents the subdivision of the Law of Three which becomes heavier the further it moves from the primordial *prakriti*. Three *gunas* are added in each world to the sum of *gunas* from the preceding world.

3 — 3 *gunas* of primordial *prakriti.*

6 — $3 + 3 = 6 + 3 = 9$

12 — $9 + 3 = 12 + 9 = 21$

24 — $21 + 3 = 24 + 21 = 45$

48 — $45 + 3 = 48 + 45 = 93$

96 — $93 + 3 = 96 + 93 = 189$

192 — $189 + 3 = 192, \ldots$

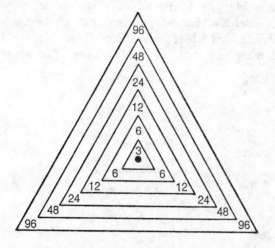

The triangle shows how three broken lines enclose a surface. This surface has two dimensions, but there is a third dimension to be reached, in conformity with a Vedic law indicating three successive stages. They follow one another in the manner indicated below:

1. The stage in which the potter's wheel sets up a circular movement.

2. The stage when the clay placed on the wheel becomes malleable; the circular movement gives a form to the clay, but the latter still remains on the same level.

3. The stage when a spindle is fixed on the wheel. The clay at once comes up in a spiral. The hub will even reach a point slightly higher than the axis.

This movement explains why there are moments of progression in life and moments of regression and time which elapses between these different movements. In spiritual experience, every man ought to aspire to raise himself around an axis, and every woman to become a perfect triangle to create perfect forms.

In the following diagram the seeker stands between two triangles. He who devotes his life to spiritual search, thanks to his inner discipline, absorbs the *Shakti* of the triangle of the infinite ideal which is above him. Below him the downward triangle contains all possible forms of manifestation.

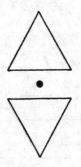

Perfect *yoga* in the heart of life is represented by the two integrated triangles with a single center. A Master is one who voluntarily enters into *prakriti*. His disciples and pupils are so many reflections of himself which he recognizes without being attached to them. He stands in the center of the two triangles.

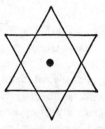

The imagery of the triangle, in Tantric esotericism pictures the *Shakti* as the water chestnut (*shringâtaka*), a peculiar pyramid-shaped fruit growing in swamps. There again you have the idea of density.

The radiation of energy has two movements, one of them centripetal and the other centrifugal. The interaction of these two movements produces the luminous sphere of all existence, technically known as *bindu*, which is situated in the center of the pyramid. Creation may appear and start from any point, moving either from the center outwards, or from the periphery towards the center. *Shakti* never stops creating, whether she unfolds or gathers herself in. In fact, both these movements are complementary, just as are the phenomena of denseness and rarefaction.

What we need is to break the inertia that hinders or slows the passage from one stage to another. I use the word *tapasya* in speaking of this movement, and the instantaneous power of transformation whether it be centripetal or centrifugal.

The *Vedas* tell us that we have a "Father in Heaven" and a "Mother on Earth." They are linked together by the atmosphere full of clouds, full of quarrels between the gods and quarrels between the demons, full of book knowledge and all the philosophies of life. The *Shastras* and the *Purânas* bind us with chains called spirituality, orthodoxy, politics, castes, and economy.

What does man possess that could eventually free him? As often as not he is unaware of it, for *prakriti* jealously holds him under her sway. And yet most of his instinctive movements are right. His original, very primitive nature can serve him in his thought as in his feelings. And this is his chance, for he will gradually discover in himself a spiritual strength which will lead him to worship the divine Mother in one or another of her aspects, and an animal force through which he will identify himself with one of the Mother's divine vehicles: tiger, swan, peacock, cat.

The cosmic laws act on the level of our understanding, but we are able to perceive only a very few of them. As a result, we can adapt the conditions of our life only to those laws we have recognized. The cosmic laws operate in time. And the notion of time, beyond our limitations, is unknown to us. What consciousness of time do people in India have? Their concept will seem to you difficult to understand until you integrate it in yourself.

The *Tantras* indicate a method to realize the zero value of time. Technically, this value is called *bindu*. It is said that the pronunciation of a sacred formula (*mantra*) takes three *moras* and a half. The half is the point (*bindu*) which contains the all and is attained by drawing in the consciousness through seven stages, each stage in a geometric progression with different intervals: $\frac{1}{2} + (\frac{1}{4} \ldots \frac{1}{8} \ldots \frac{1}{16} \ldots \frac{1}{32} \ldots \frac{1}{64} \ldots \frac{1}{128} \ldots \frac{1}{256}) \ldots$ of a mora.

In reality, this is the alternating movement of consciousness in an inner concentration lasting as long as the recitation of the *japa* (sacred formulas) until one comes in contact with the Void. This *bindu*, more subtle than the atom, and Brahman, "the Vaster than the vast" are the same. Both are the Void. Time moves between the two. Between the two, there are the coils of manifestation like the coils of a serpent. The serpent is the innate force (*Shakti*). This innate force, also called *kundalinî*, is the operative force between the two modes of the Void.

V

Masters and Disciples

The disciples in an *âshram* are attracted not by pure meta-physical research, but by the person of the Guru, who for them becomes the light on the path, the ideal made concrete. The rule of "loyalty to the Guru" immediately comes into play. The Guru's authority (Gurudom) is boundless.

Traditionally, the Guru's unspoken promise to his disciple is as follows: "I am here to lead you toward liberation. Do my work obediently and you will be saved. You will know the highest ecstasy and will be freed from the round of births and deaths (*samsâra*). If I go to heaven, you will come to heaven with me; if I go to hell, you will come to hell with me."

The Guru's responsibility is immense; he shoulders the *karma* of all those around him. For their part, the disciples are happy to throw their *karma* on his back. Is there a Master great enough to wish that his disciple will "stand one day on his shoulder"? If he does not have the thought "one day my disciple will be more famous than I," right away a descending law operates. Owing to the Guru's hold over his disciple, there is often something morbid in their relationship, like that of father to son when the son is doomed to remain a son without ever becoming a father.

In the preliminary part of the *Sâmkhya* discipline, the relationship of disciple to Guru is compared to a seed buried in the earth. The seed is left to develop on its own in the heart of what feeds it; it absorbs the Guru. It will become a strong plant, bearing foliage, flowers, fruit, and seeds. In so doing, it transcends the ground in which it grew and becomes directly responsible to Great Nature for the life it contains. *Sâmkhya*, the Guru, is carried by it.

An attitude particularly conducive to rapid progress is that of total obedience to the Guru in all things: thoughts, attitudes, and actions. The aim is to become the "well-tilled soil" the Master needs. As everyone knows from Indian tradition, with rare exceptions this field, plowed with such care, will only be used in a future life when the right impulse will take possession of it. Slow and deep preparation is most important.

Great is the illusion of the man who believes that he can reach the goal after a few months of efforts! His ambition will be stopped at precisely the point where he becomes conscious of his personal fate (*svadharma*), of his own law as it operates in the midst of cosmic laws. This is equivalent to discovering the Divine living in the heart, to serve it, to worship it, but nothing more. A wild rosebush can be forced to produce big flowers of its kind, but a wild rosebush will never be able to produce anything but wild roses; any grafting promised by a Guru would mean that he is an impostor. And pseudo-Gurus are legion! This moment of becoming self-conscious is the crucial point. It means the death of the illusory ideal and often brings violent reactions. But should the ideal be interiorized, that moment of consciousness is a moment of understanding. There is no idea of perfection in this ideal, but rather a feeling of unity on that level of understanding. Here we touch the very heart of the living power.

A Guru and his disciple are like a mother and child—joined together by an umbilical cord. There is no tension whatsoever in this attachment. If there was tension, it would mean that the "psychic being," which has to grow between them and develop until it becomes the "heat" of their blood, would never be formed for lack of the necessary substance.

If it is born, it must be fed and cared for. It is both "cause and effect," meaning that it exists out of time. That is the reason why there is no longer any "why" or "how" in a rightly established relationship between Guru and disciple. Master and disciple can each say to the other, "I am you . . ." The same vibration animates them. The "child" between them may disappear one day, when certain vibrations mathematically reach a known point of resorption. Then, Life in its totality becomes the Guru.

There are four kinds of devotees:

1. He who becomes a devotee because he is in danger.

2. He who wants grace, help, health, security from the Master, or simply to live close to him for his own sake.

3. He who has a thirst for knowledge. In such a case, the Master's physical person and way of life are of little importance to him.

4. He who *knows* without being aware of it, who by nature is good soil. Such a devotee is the best of all, welcoming obstacles on his path because they increase his determination. He has his own roots. For him, what matters is to live an experience, no matter how difficult.

Does a Master care for such a devotee? The answer is illustrated by the story of Lord Nârâyan who one day was resting after having stationed two faithful watchmen at his door, Jaya (Victory) and Vijaya (total Victory), to drive off intruders. Four *Rishis* arrive from afar and ask to see Nârâyan. A violent quarrel breaks out at the door of the god, the *Rishis* curse the two watchmen. Awakened by the noise, Lord Nârâyan appears, bowing to the *Rishis;* at the same time he is also deeply upset, for nothing can erase the curse the *Rishis* have called down. It must take effect. Nârâyan says to his two faithful watchmen, "Since you have been cursed, as beings you must enter the round of births and deaths, but I can allow you to choose your fate. Do you wish to be born among my devotees or among my enemies?"

"What difference will it make?" ask Jaya and Vijaya.

"If you are among my devotees, it will take you seven lives to reach me; if you are among my enemies, it will only take you three!"

And so it happened that Jaya and Vijaya willingly became great enemies of Nârâyan, constantly hating and therefore constantly remembering the god. One of them became Râvana[1] who was killed by Râma.

Devotees asleep in devotion and self-satisfaction avoid obstacles that might awaken them. What courage it takes to create the very obstacle which would bring them closer to the Divine!

The relationship between Master and disciple is established by an infallible law, with a view to the esoteric transmission of the cosmic laws and their operation. Once this relationship is clearly established, one can neither break out of it nor make decisions for oneself nor sidestep the law once it has been recognized and one's part in it discovered. That would only be mental self-deception.

[1] A fearsome demon, King of Lanka, who had carried off Sîtâ.

What is most difficult is the surrender of the mind because until a real birth takes place on a different plane, this surrender appears as a state of alarming torpor. This state of passivity is always painful.

During all this period there is a deep contrast between the subjective attachment of the disciple to the Guru and the objective love of the Guru for his disciple. What the Master can transmit is not an idea nor a form, but a means. The *Kaushitaki Upanishad*[2] describes the traditional way in which the dying "father" passes on his power to his "son."

It can be compared to the passing on of power from Guru to disciple: "Let me put into you my word, my breath, and my vision; what I perceive, what I taste, likewise my actions, pains and pleasures, the concepts to which I have been attached, and my search itself. In you I place my spirit and my consciousness. I give you the breath of my life (*prânâ*). May power, sanctity and honors go with you . . ." The son or disciple answers, "May your words be fulfilled . . . Go in peace!"

In the life of Buddha, this moment is when he set the wheel of the law in motion of those around him, saying, "Go, speak of the law for the benefit of many. When the soil is tilled sow one seed of knowledge in it, no more, and go on further."

Every Guru has only a very few key ideas at the root of his teaching. These ideas are the ones that brought him to realization. No others. He will constantly bring his teaching back to the fruits of his personal efforts which keep his spiritual experience alive.

Some Masters try to express these ideas by a single key word, others purposely dilute them in order to pass them on to a larger number of disciples. So there are two methods, that of interiorization and that of exteriorization, which the ortho-

[2] 2.15.

dox Hindu at once recognizes. Both of them are traditional. Both of them demand a total sacrifice and cost dearly.

No Master transmits the totality of what he has received, but only what he has assimilated. As a result, once the Master consciously acts in accordance with the laws known to him, he manipulates them like chemical formulas, transmitting fragments to those around him. On the other hand, no fragment of knowledge is ever transmitted before the disciple has perceived it or had an inkling of it. In short, the Master is merely an indispensable intermediary between the laws and those who are ready to discover them.

There are great Masters and small Masters. Both of them do exactly the same work, for great Masters are for great disciples and small Masters for small disciples. The relationship between Master and disciple is the same in both cases.

What is important to the Master, after having consciously reached the zenith of his upward curve, is to see the downward curve with equal consciousness and to choose the point from which he will teach. This point will keep constantly moving in response to his own active search.

In their childishness, and because of their competitive spirit, disciples are always anxious to discover the sources from which their Master has drawn his knowledge. Some of them ask questions and discuss them; others demand proof and argue. And what do they find? Nothing worthwhile, for the Master transmits what has become his own substance. It is through this substance that the disciple will taste what he is able to assimilate, of the law.

Every saint or Guru speaks according to a "principle," adopted and faithfully served, in which lives a hidden truth. The Guru is perfectly aware of this. This fragment of truth belonging to ultimate reality is the only thing of real value, whereas the principle in itself, on the human level, merely tends to create the form of a discipline.

A Master teaches never more than a tenth of what he knows. In like manner, air is only a tenth part of ether, and water only a tenth part of air, and so forth. It cannot be otherwise. The Master cannot allow his strength to be further reduced. This explains why there is such a rapid degradation between the level of the Guru and that of the third generation of his disciples. A well-known cosmic law comes into play here.

Some of the sacred formulas (*mantras*) have been revealed and commentaries on them exist. Their form is known, even to the number of vibrations in each letter. But only the Guru knows their *bîjas*[3] and these he never reveals. Were he to do so, he himself would come to resemble an empty vessel.

It is really of no importance whether the death of the Guru occurs after he has given his seed or after he has allowed it to be reabsorbed in himself, for the disciple who is a Master by nature will have found by himself the correct resonance of his Guru's *bîja*. In the *Tantras*, the *mantra* has four forms. The first is given in detail (*stotra*) as in a hymn. Then this detailed form is condensed into a one-sentence formula (*mâlâ*). This condensed form in its turn will become a single word (*nâma*). And lastly, this subtle form, which is no more than a pure sound without meaning, is called a seed (*bîja*). The mind must be led from the hymn to the *bija*, the pure vibration that gives birth to the psychic body of the disciple.

No matter what stage he has reached, a disciple must learn not to talk about what he has received. All experiences, spectacular and fleeting, are no more than the vision of the level he is trying to reach. To believe in them and talk about them would be a pure illusion of the ego. Because of this, a period of silence after each experience is a wise measure of protection.

The seeker goes his way, driven by an inner hunger, until

3 See p. 122.

he finds the Guru who will accept him and tell him what discipline to follow. Sometimes, faced with a difficulty of understanding, the disciple blames this on his Guru and goes away; he is driven downward without being aware of it, caught by the law of gravity. And so he becomes a parasite in the spiritual search, fed by his ego.

When the time comes, every great Guru drives away, from himself and from those close to him, the disciple to whom over a long period he has given a great deal. He refuses to allow his pupil any opportunity to enter his life or to imitate him in any way. He expels him when he is ready by giving him a task, for "there cannot be two tigers in the same forest."

The disciple who is told to leave is fundamentally different from the disciples who remain to live under the direct inspiration of the Master. He takes away with him a seed to be sown where he goes. He leaves without anyone knowing, having secretly received from the Master the "gift of the power" which will be his support in life.

This is the origin of the traditional roaming about. The one who goes away changes his name. His trace is lost. No one asks about him. On the lower vital plane, the wildcat, when the right time comes, drives her kittens away from her. At the risk of their lives, they must find their own territory and hunting ground.

The independent disciple possesses nothing. He only belongs to what is real, for he has been fed by the Guru's essence. Either he will grow and develop with fresh vigor because of the very severance he has lived and the difficulties that await him, or he will perish unheard of. In the latter case, he becomes humus fertilizing *prakriti*, a humus with a definite function to fulfill, however humble.

But most of a Master's disciples remain close to him all their lives. They are a necessity for the Guru, just as the presence of the Guru is a necessity for them. These disciples have a role to fill. They are the fine matter which the Master uses to manifest his work in *prakriti*. Without them, the Master would be merely a radiance, but through their presence these disciples fix the circle in which the Master's vibrations create the ferment of possible evolution.

Until the disciple assumes his responsibilities, the Master's stomach works and digests for him, but the disciple continues to question his Master: "Who are you?" Krishnamurti answers, "I have never read any sacred books." The disciples of Mâ Ananda Moyî cut one off with the words, "She has never received anything from anyone, since she already knew everything when she was born," even though they themselves have put forth the same question a hundred times! The same question has also been asked about Gurdjieff. One could answer with another question, "Who can tell what the Pathans, that proud people of the Northern Frontier, are made of?" They were originally Aryans who became Muslims after having been Buddhist; but above all, they are to this day the sturdy children of their own land. In a like manner, just as the river Triveni at Allahabad unites three sources, so the knowledge of Gurdjieff has at least three different sources in the East— Vedism, Buddhism, and Islam.

Gurdjieff was, of course, a real *charvaka*, that is to say, a rebel against learnedly expounded orthodoxies that constrict the mind. He behaved like all the mystics and powerful Gurus who, at a given moment, have called the crowds to them. In the same way, Shrî Râmakrishna in his exaltation climbed to the roof of the temple at Dakshineshvar near Calcutta and, weeping, cried out, "Come to me from everywhere, disciples, so that I may teach you. I am ready!" Others, like Shrî Râmana Maharshi, through their silence and absorption have forced those who approached him to ask themselves the question, "Who am I?" Some of these *charvakas* have found fame without looking for it. Some have continued to roam about; others have allowed followers to gather around them. Still others have repeatedly fled from the slavery created by the excessive solicitude of their disciples. Still others have accepted this bondage with a definite aim known to them alone. Many of them have lived incognito in the midst of the world, hidden in the crowd, and have died without leaving any apparent trace. Since the *charvakas* have never been written about, it is only indirectly, thanks to the reactions they arouse, that their name circulated by word of mouth. Their freedom and influence have been so great that orthodox people in every tradition have pursued and persecuted them.

Should one attempt to say what *charvakas* are? It is written that their ancestor was Brihaspati, a Vedic sage. Fragments of their teachings are scattered throughout the *Katha Upanishad*, the *Mahâbhârata*, and the Buddhist writings. In the days of the Buddha, people listened attentively to their voice, but their enemies gave such a distorted description of their positive, antiritualist philosophy centered on the search for the "I" that later they hid their well-guarded secret, the mastery of one of the paths leading to knowledge.

There is an enormous disparity between quality and quantity; quality hides within, whereas quantity spreads outward.

He who possesses the gift of captivating the imagination of the many and of transforming it into creative imagination is a born Guru. When using a lamp, its light loses none of its brilliance, but when one takes a pound of sugar out of a bag, it leaves an empty space in the mass of material. When receiving the *darshan*[4] of a Master, one touches the spirit itself, but as soon as one makes arrangements to stay close to

[4] To be in the presence of a Master, to be seen by him; the establishment of a current between Master and disciple.

him, the "downward curve" begins and the law of gravity im-
mobilizes the spirit.

One cannot escape from this law, nor from its process of
materialization. Owing to its constantly moving densities, matter will always be either somewhat more or somewhat less
receptive to spirit.

The Guru sees what is happening with an intelligence that
is not the intelligence of his disciples. He dwells at the center
of an esoteric circle which, of course, carries its own limitations; but this circle is far above the circle in which the
disciples move.

In comparison with them, he is living in knowledge.

However, the Guru is well aware that this knowledge is
relative, and that he himself is a seeker in relation to knowledge existing in the circle above him. A Guru arriving at the
end of his search would be an impostor; a disciple who is a
fanatic will satisfy himself by imagining that his Guru has
reached the end, thus cutting himself off from the laws, from
the ascending and descending movements that support life.

Why would you want the moment of knowledge to last?
Even Brahmâ cannot keep for himself what he creates! Everything springs from him and at once flows out. Ten million
gods or laws at once take possession of it. We are a humble
part of those who are trying to swim upstream. And what do
we find? Close by we hear the repeated calls of Krishnamurti
who is becoming impatient, for, despite the shocks he creates,
Great Nature does not transform itself. He halts those caught
in the circumstances of life and shouts, "Stop! Understand
who you are! Understand what you are doing!"

Elsewhere, in the sphere she governs, the Mother of Shrî
Aurobindo's *âshram* declares, "O Nature, material Mother,
you said that you would collaborate in the transformation of
man; there is no limit to the splendor of such collaboration."

The unfolding of time here enters into play, in the very play of *prakriti*.

Mâ Ananda Moyî, was the first in history, faithful to the Buddhist tradition still widespread in Bengal, to roam about Northern India, stopping only to sleep and eat in temple resthouses. For years she lived almost continually in ecstasy without any relationship with her surroundings, completely cut off from the rhythm of Nature. She returned gradually to the human state, at first unconsciously through a known process. Now she has voluntarily returned to the rhythm of *prakriti* to transmit her experience to those around her and teach a way of possible expansion.

And what has Gurdjieff, with his broad shoulders, created for you in the West? Surely a field of *prakriti* corresponding to your own possibilities. This *prakriti* is arranged with care to offer you many toys, instruments to use, and all kinds of "intelligent absurdities," which you wish to keep in your hands, hide in a strongbox, or piously preserve in memory because you love to possess things. This same *prakriti* will also reveal to you the many steps to climb to approach the goal without depriving you of all the possible ways to break your neck!

In all these circumstances, what tools will the Master use? The ones that suit him best. What difference is there between a bare room like the one in which we are speaking together and a room filled with a hodgepodge like a bazaar? The Master utilizes the means that are needed to bring his disciple to him. Some day perhaps, if such is his wish and need, he will take the very bones of his disciple, crush them, and offer them to the gods in a pie. He has the right to make use of the trust the disciple has placed in him, his surrender, and even the essence of his being (*bhûta*) to the uttermost limits.

So what remains of the disciple, once his bones have been crushed? Nothing. For him it is death. There are deliberate

deaths in which the blood flows, as in many temple sacrifices where the bodies of the decapitated goats keep on
jumping and twitching after life departs. What is it that is
freed by death? There is also the secret death of dogs, branded
as they are by the curse of impurity, who hide under a bush
to die with a dignity the *sannyâsins* covet and hope to have
at the moment of their own death. One of the hardest com-
mandments in the initiation into *sannyâsa* is "When the day
comes, know how to die like the dog, with dignity, unnoticed."

Does the disciple know that by his death he is serving the
"essence of the Guru?" Impossible! Can ashes know what
use they have? If he so desires, the Guru can swallow up his
disciple; he has the right to do it. He can use the liberated
energy, just as we eat the food we need. The interdependence
of functions is a fact; it is right and normal. And why should
it be otherwise? The *Gîtâ* states clearly how few out of a
million pass through the narrow gate. But the aspiration is
there. How can we know what is above us, since we only
control the relationship of the planes of consciousness that
we have discovered and acquired? That is why death in the
"Guru's essence" is the highest goal we can desire. We cannot
lift our *prakriti* higher. The best we can do, in all our reactions, is to let the raw material of our nature be united with
the movements of the spirit and to place these reactions in the
heart—the heart that may become the "seat of the Guru"
(*gadi*). This movement in itself is the voluntary death of the
ego. It is only in this voluntary death that the Guru sees what
is permanent in us, what really exists in the fact of Being
(*Sat*). Only he can give it form and life. In this he is like
the Creator in Genesis taking one of Adam's ribs to free the
divine *Shakti* who is ready to give birth. Without this shock
coming from above, no transformation is possible.

Another transformation is to give birth in ourselves to

Shakti's child. This child will grow up in a different *pra-kriti*—different in quality. Right away the child will call for a plaything. He must hold something in his hands to have the pleasure of throwing it on the ground, to pick it up and give it away, to take it back. He does it without any logic in his movements, just to move around and discover what life is. So always surround yourself with plenty of toys—for yourself and for others.

VI.

Method and Teaching

How can one conceive of pure Existence (*Sat*) in the heart of life? A characteristic feature of thought is to transmute the concrete into the abstract; in the end, thought is interested only in the abstract. It is a kind of escape. The relation with life is then simply cut off. But when man, impelled by his self-esteem, resolutely looks into himself, he resists the temptation to be carried away by the abstract.

In this domain, the energy that has been withdrawn from the outer field will quite naturally become more intense as it reaches the inner field. But if this intensity is merely the repercussion of a shock coming from life in the world, it can devastate the field of consciousness. Having been damaged, consciousness no longer has any aim. If this intensity is skillfully cultivated, it can lead to the perception of pure Existence

(*Sat*), in which the polarity between subject and object is resolved in a feeling of identity.

The experience in which the dualities arising from the polarity of consciousness cease through natural absorption lies beyond all other experiences in a state of quietude, even in the midst of life. It is a creative matrix which gives birth to new forms when the old forms are used up. This is an important experience even in its very early stages. During a certain period the need for quietude can be dominant, and to attribute to it a negative value would be to disregard the very rhythm of nature. It would be more accurate to see it as the prelude to a need to create. It is true that when a pupil plunges into himself, his force appears to be lost. This force will reappear, but where and when? This is precisely the time when the Guru gives active protection and support to his disciple.

We look on confidently at all the movements of interiorized consciousness. It seems to be passive, inert, like dead matter, but actually it is a living force with a quite definite quality of feeling. In this respect, a perception has to be evaluated according to the quality of energy it frees in the realm of feeling and in the realm of will. In the realm of will, it becomes dispassionate and disinterested action, and in that of feeling it becomes the sublimation of the basic emotions of the heart.

In practice, quietude easily appears like a high place from which to face life's problems, and the technique to be followed consists in counterbalancing every positive energy with a negative energy, knowing that both are in the Void. Without deviation, consciousness takes a direction that it will maintain. Along the way its awareness is able to transform the emotional movements it encounters. One can speak of the absorption of shocks through an absence of inner resistance. This is not inactivity, for will is present, operating in time with a clear vision of what reality is. This vision (*kavikratu*) has already been described by the Vedic sages.

The "space-time" concept of the *Upanishads* has become the dimension of existence in which everything "moves without movement," for all movement finally is merely the displacement of what is contained in a seed—a seed that is self-sufficient and able, if it chooses, to withdraw into itself. Thus, a seed of thought that, at every instant of its development, can intensify all its energies in perceiving its existence, has no necessity to evolve. And yet does evolve! Therein lies the mystery beyond intellect, the static state of pure Existence (*Sat*) in life.

In the *Shâstras* there is an oft-repeated precept that one should never speak unnecessarily of one's spiritual experiences. If you do so, it shows that you have nothing yet in your own being that is valid and able to preserve the current of power which has come down to you. He who readily talks about himself is like a little child who runs to his mother to tell her about everything he came across while he was playing.

Before you speak about an experience, you must learn to observe it in silence for a long time. First, it has to find its place in you, be distilled, and bear fruit. In short, it must become yours. While this is going on, life is reduced to a few movements and a very few expressed thoughts.

The "Great Manu"[1] taught three important rules which should never be forgotten: "Speak only when you are questioned. If you are asked an illogical question, or if you detect a hidden motive in it, remain silent. Keep silent among fools; play with them on their level."

Never uphold your personal ideas in discussion with a saint,

---

[1] The person thought to be the father of the human race. He is credited with a code of laws which has retained considerable authority up to the present day.

a wise man, a *pandit*, nor with a Brahmin who knows the *Vedas*, nor yet with your parents.

The yogi's role is not to be a savior of souls; but by the fact of persistently working on his ego, he forces a resistance that will open our eyes to our own egos.

When one has consciously set out on the path of search, there is no turning back. It is as though one were intoxicated. But the impetus of the start is often slowed down by all the heavy and useless burdens we carry with us.

In the episode of the *Avadhûta*[2] the crow tells a story: "I was flying with a piece of meat in my beak. Twenty crows were chasing me and quarreling, trying to grab it. I had to fly high and fool them. I was weary. Suddenly, I dropped the piece of meat and saw the twenty crows gliding down after it with loud cawings and fighting over it. Then I shook my wings. How wonderful it felt not to have anything to carry. All the sky belonged to me!"

Every spiritual discipline is a detailed work. After a period of conscious efforts, there is always a period of temporary retreat, of "cave life," to attain mastery over disorderly movements of *prakriti* which defends itself and attacks in a cunning way. We should not talk about our force. It remains a secret.

During this period three rules should be followed:

1. Be humble to disarm that which resists.
2. Accept everything.
3. Be intimate with no one.

If these three rules are respected, the "abstract sound" of the effort will remain pure.

The couch grass that has invaded a field causes great havoc. In the same way, man's objective vision, even if fragmentary, works on him and cannot be uprooted. Once one has learned

---

[2] Book XI, chapters 7–10 of the *Bhâgavatapurâna*, a vast treatise probably dating from the sixth century.

to see, one can no longer live like a blind man. Every question, whatever it is, carries its own answer and reveals the prison of him who asks it. The Master touches the sensitive point where the freedom he reveals and the darkness of the disciple confront one another. Or put in another way, where the liberty of the disciple who is advancing comes up against the discipline demanded by the Guru, that discipline appears like a prison.

An unusual quality of courage is needed to follow the advice, "Rely only on yourself!" This is the same as saying, "Isolate the direct experience you are living until it becomes a part of you. Do not reveal it until you are able to connect it with something known and precise."

The difficulty arises from the fact that one is surrounded by other disciples on the same way, each of whom remains enclosed in concern for his own personal discipline. Everyone is working on his own. The same holds true for the gods. In every temple, each god is seated on his lotus flower. The gods are the permanent supports of a certain effort, whereas the individual efforts of disciples have only momentary stability.

If you ask a disciple or a co-disciple to help you, he will stay by you, but if you are not going his way, he will strictly exclude you from his thoughts. At any moment you risk feeling rejected by the group. To pass from one level of understanding to another is equivalent to a surgical operation. Many lack the courage to get over the obstacles that await them and "ossify" their base in order not to see them, which gives them a rock of certainty to hang onto. From then on, such disciples are always talking about their sincerity as being an essential quality of *yoga*, whereas the man who is daring enough to look the law full in the face is the one who makes the "spiritual discovery."

There is in man such anguish, such dissatisfaction with himself that even if he had thousands of words at his disposal, they would not suffice to express it. His pursuit of all the things from which he seeks some solace will never bring him the calm that he desires. And how could it be otherwise? Every path he follows is thorny. Disgusted by the difficulties, he abandons one path after another. Until he awakens to himself and realizes that he is in fact the owner of his own field, he will never acquire the plowshare and the plow with which to till it.[3] While meditating, one is often tempted either to force the mind to pursue a definite line or to get rid of the influx of thoughts. However, the only correct effort is to harmonize the waves of impressions with the indispensable plane of peace.

The ritual of the *Vaishnavites*, the worshipers of Vishnu, gives valuable indications on this subject: instead of torturing the mind in order to make it pass through the eye of a needle, one must draw to oneself the full "life of the body" and the entire "consciousness of the body" to serve the Divine in its particular aspect (*Ishta*), to receive Him, to surround Him, to worship Him. Thus, little by little, a unity of consciousness is established, which makes use of all the levels of the being and all conscious and unconscious efforts. Then peace and impressions become one.

In spiritual discipline, movements of attraction and repulsion are normal until such time as one reaches a certain balance. Four levels have to be passed through to reach the concept of the Void:

1. Primordial ignorance.
2. The plane of the ego that is matrix of *prakriti* with pleasure and pain in all their forms.
3. The "I" that makes it possible to observe oneself.
4. The Void that is everything and nothing.

Primitive man in darkness (*tamas*) is very close to animal instincts, very close to the earth with a consciousness not

[3] An allusion to King Janaka, p. 112.

awakened. For him to have reached the plane of the ego is an achievement in which he will remain for a long time, perhaps for several successive lives, before an impulse of another order arises. Only a very slow development is allowed by nature. She is more inclined to favor a change of species than a change of consciousness.

The idea of "returning"[4] to the point where, for the first time, an act of conscious will has given a direction to the current of life is one of the great *Sâmkhya* disciplines. This discipline proposes through methodical observation to follow the path of thought "backwards" as well as in the normal flow. Then we perceive that the only "food" or "substances" that have permanent value are those that issue from the essence of the being, whereas everything that has come from outside has almost been obliterated. To find again this point is equivalent to seeing clearly when and how our personal destiny (*dharma*) is formed. Each time it takes place, it produces a shock which makes a step forward possible.

Spirit and matter are two different aspects of the same reality. Every creation is generated in the Void. The same is true of the stress engendered in the equipotential field of energy. Stress creates the feeling of a fullness we term body or matter.

Thus, on the one hand, the body is nothing but the fulfillment of the spirit. On the other hand, one may say that spirit is like the glow of the body when it is burning with its own energy. Automatic combustion of the body is life. Heat turns into light. So there is a complete parallelism:

matter—heat—light
body —life —spirit

[4] To return to what is basically primitive; see pp. 89f.

If you approach reality from the spirit and come down to the body, you are following the teaching of *Sâmkhya*. If you rise from the body to the spirit, you are a yogi. But if, with an awake attention, you perceive clearly the interrelation between the descending and ascending movements, you can work in both ways. Then you are on the path of Tantrism. May you one day pursue a true Tantric discipline in the broadest and grandest meaning of the word.

Certainly the most authentic picture of Shrî Râmakrishna is the one given by Swâmi Vivekânanda who saw the "man" in him. If Shrî Râmakrishna submitted to a Tantric discipline for nine years, it was in order to escape from imprisonment within himself caused by the notions of "good" and "evil" in order later to make free use of them.

For those who only saw Shrî Râmakrishna at the end of his life, it is easy to maintain that he was born in a state of grace and followed no *yoga* except to show the way; hence the assertion expressed in a meeting of *pandits* that he was an incarnation, an *avatar*. This is to ignore the entire Tantric period of his life, just as there are many years in the life of Christ that are unknown.

His wife Sâradâ Devî never gave the impression of having separated herself from humanity. Shrî Râmakrishna was reflected in her. After his death Sâradâ Devî was surrounded by veneration in which sentiment had a larger place than objectivity. However, she remained "outside" in contact with life, in a state of consciousness induced by her creative imagination. Shrî Râmakrishna spoke a great deal, Sâradâ Devî hardly at all.

The seated position (*âsana*) is for each of us the one we naturally re-assume to "come back to ourselves." In this position there is no tension. The body is flexible. In myself I find again the form of myself which is well known to me in every detail, for there nothing is left to unknown chance. I am seated quietly, my spinal column erect. I am looking straight ahead. Even if at first my eyes are closed, they continue to look straight ahead.

I know how I sit, how I get up, how I walk, how I hold my head and use my hands. Each of these movements is in itself a personal *âsana*, or a voluntary movement connected with the *âsana* that helps me to collect myself in a quiet moment. Everything is related to the dignity of my inner being. In life, the person that I am uses the body for the role the person has to play. This body is my instrument and my vehicle; my first duty is to care for it. Each gesture takes place by itself in a moment of interiorization without the intervention of the will or of thought.

There is much to be said about the secret role of the three "locks" of the body. A certain automatism must be gradually acquired so as to preserve one's force and energy during moments of interiorization. This has to do with an automatic system of detection for catching any kind of contraction since the slightest tension is an indication of a wrong direction.

1. When all contractions of the body and the mind have ceased, the chin will tilt towards the chest. This movement happens of itself; it corresponds to a certain letting go of tension in the spinal column, which undoes the knots of the nerves. Then the abdomen spontaneously becomes concave. These two movements are so nearly simultaneous that they are practically one.

2. A second automatic movement follows: the extension of the chest, without any hardening. This position leads of itself to the following state.

3. Without any voluntary movement, without any contraction, the anus closes giving to energy an upward direction. The closed anus is the nadir point of a current that must be maintained. If this "lock" is not closed, the inner body will

gradually be invaded by depressive and negative emotions that have no connection with the realm of true sensation.

When a perfect chord vibrates between Master and disciple, a continuous conversation proceeds between them without any words being uttered. This takes place even without inner dialogue. At this stage the function of speech is no longer activated because the inner organs (*indriyas*), which join the five sense organs to their objects, no longer play a role.

On both sides, communication then becomes pure vibration. One of the conditions of this state is to be able to think without words. So long as words or any formulation arise in thought or in prayer, it means that this vibration, which is in itself creative, is not taking place.

One way of minimizing the consciousness of the ego is the constant repetition of a sacred word (*mantra*), consciously at first, then very rapidly, in a mechanical and unconscious way (*japa*). On the other hand, there is the voluntary discipline of silence—one or two fixed hours during the day, or a whole day each week, leading by stages to that inner silence which is one of the most delicate disciplines.

The vibration of thought and of speech without words has no connection with telepathy. On a certain level this vibration exists between Master and disciple because they share the same vision.

What inner silence does is to touch the seed of thought that is the only way to return to the initial movement of the inner organs of perception; then everything around you fades away of itself. It is a strange mode of perception in which the will does not interfere. The voluntary stopping of thought leads to direct contact with the initial point where the basic note of all known harmonics resounds.

Thus we come to a very few thoughts, through which, as it is said in Sanskrit, one single "sound" says many things.

For instance, "*â*" means: come, enter, approach, hold what I give you; "*yâ*" means: go out, it is finished, this is not the moment. Thus, between silence and a plethora of words, one could live with some ten syllables in whose vibrations it would be possible to understand languages one does not know.

In the same order of ideas, it is astonishing to see that the questions put to a Master are all alike. If Shrî Râmana Maharshi lived for so long amidst his own people without speaking, it is because his basic note responded to all the vibrations of the people around him.

Gurdjieff often speaks about the plurality of "I's." In substance he says, "Bring all the 'I's' to the 'I' of essence, knowing in advance that in the place of essence you may find an 'I' who will try to fool you!"

At the start, the "I" towards which all the "I's" converge is only theoretically the Void. Through your present discipline you draw close to an "I" from which you can calmly observe yourself. From there the world is seen with all its mechanical movements; from there a glimpse of that "I" which is the Void may appear.

The next stage cannot be taught by any book. It must be lived degree by degree, with the Master holding one's hand. It is the slow discovery that finally there is no "I" but only that "which is active" in you. At that moment something may take place, but the attention is so delicate that the least movement can destroy it even though the attention is there, both inside and outside. We feel it and see it at the same time. We also see the mechanism of all those things that come from nowhere and go nowhere. If we do not see this in its marvelous aspect, we have an impression of self-extinction. If, suddenly, we find ourselves in the midst of the unexpected miracles where the movement of *prakriti* ceases for an instant, we are totally "one" with an impression of life, of heat.

At that moment, I am seized by a deep feeling of dissociation. "I am not here. I am not there. Where am I?" Anguish could grip me, but a readjustment is certain—I have only to wait for it, I know that it will happen; as it is automatic, I can trust it! I shall find myself again face to face with *prakriti* and can "play" with her and take part in the movement of manifestation. In that instant, the ego will have vanished.

The Void exists. It matters little to the Void whether *prakriti* exists or not. Two Indian terms make this clear: *pudgala nairâtmya*, the Void within the ego, and *dharma nairâtmya*, the Void of the twelve, twenty-four, and forty-eight cosmic laws. Having arrived at this point of comprehension, it is possible to see how *prakriti* works.

Tantric teaching demonstrates that all life is born from the Void—the gods and goddesses, the higher and the lower *prakriti*. The Void is the matrix of universal energy.

One has access to it by four stages. In his book *In Search of the Miraculous*, Ouspensky speaks about the first two stages. He remained silent about the last two because he had left Gurdjieff. In all of his subsequent personal teaching, which is very important, he tells of the development of these two first stages and of his experiences with his Master. The writings of Gurdjieff,[5] on the other hand, open for us the frontiers of the two last stages. These are cleverly hidden in his mythical narrations. The four stages are: plurality of "I's," a single "I," no "I," the Void.

At the moment something takes place, it is difficult to realize that it would inevitably have taken place. We are loath to admit that for *prakriti*, man, animal, plant or mineral are

[5] *All and Everything* (New York: Harcourt, Brace & Co., 1950).

merely a reserve of humus. And she needs a great deal of it. All natural cataclysms are necessities. Only the quality of the humus matters to *prakriti*. In this order of things, man plays a definite role of which he is still unconscious. Those who are becoming progressively less enslaved by nature, often possess a very refined natural intelligence. This natural intelligence knows perfectly how to make use of what is recorded by the senses and to make use of recurrences of every kind.

The first question asked by man, "Why?" brings about a considerable change. With that he becomes the enemy of *prakriti* and she defends herself. And yet, so long as he asks "Why?" he will make no progress because everything manifested in him, even in a subtle way like the spirit, is still *prakriti*, including his search and its ascending movement.

The *Vedas* mention a precise moment when the immobile has become the mobile, and another moment when the mobile has become the differentiated.

It is not possible to approach the "why" of the first cause since there is no logical answer, but the question remains as to "how" did the first movement that ever existed occur? This penetrates into the heart of the process of creation and the cosmic laws. The fineness of the sensation of real immobility of the body, which has reached a state without any tension, and the subtlety of the elements composing the multiple envelopes (*koshas*) of the psychic body make it possible for thought to become the seat of a passive experience. It may be that a certain sensation of existing is manifested, very similar to the life hidden in a seed—a power of potential Life without any apparent movement.

Even if this sensation of existing were perceived for only a fraction of a second, it would nevertheless suffice to know what took place at the instant when the "immobile" became the "mobile," or, in terms of a better-known symbol, to know what took place at the instant of the first spontaneous vibration between the two. Here one touches a definitely scientific problem in which imagination intervenes only to meet it.

He who actually goes through the experience of "non-being" in a state of deep meditation feels suddenly filled by such a surge of life that, for that very reason, the question of the "why" no longer exists for him. This surge of life is the imperative return from non-being back towards being. It is at the same time an overwhelming sensation with a recognizable taste. It is a certainty that wipes out every question.

One has evidence of this process in the certainty with which Shrî Râmakrishna gave himself up to ecstasies that sometimes lasted several days. He was quite aware that there would come a moment when this surge of life would take place. This evidently is the return to life in the envelopes of the body and the reappearance of familiar sensations while passing through all the states of consciousness.

No great yogi goes into contemplation or deep meditation before knowing with precision the laws of re-connection or, in other words, the limits of this temporary flight. He need fear no surprises, knowing as he does through experience the exact relationship between all the elements at his disposal; but for the disciples, who look after his body, the entire process naturally takes on the appearance of a miracle. The disciples only see what is happening from the outside. In fact, there is here a connection of which the yogi alone knows the exact formula. It cannot be transmitted. The reason why it cannot be communicated is that it is the result of an exact connection between pure Existence (*Sat*) and that which is of the same nature in the man who goes through the experience, namely, pure innate essence.

He who, even once in his life and for a fraction of a

second, touches that point X in which the "mobile" emerges from the "immobile," or, conversely, the point at which the "mobile" becomes the "immobile," has perceived in himself something of pure Consciousness (*Chit*). He has perceived the inconceivable, which is living! Alas, at the very moment he becomes aware of it, from fear of losing it, he gives it name and form (*nama-rupa*) under the illusion that he will be better able to find it again. And yet, what was alive has faded away, the sensation has vanished. Symbolically, this is the moment when Shiva, seeing himself for the first time in a mirror, is overjoyed by the sight of this "second," which he discovers and which becomes manifestation. This is the end of the divine solitude.

We feel rested after a night's sleep, even though this completely unconscious sleep is a return to the matrix of life. People in whom nothing is awakened literally fall asleep without knowing how to "detach" something in themselves which will remain conscious. In their heavy state of *tamas*, they are not even aware that they are asleep.

The right way to go to sleep is to do it consciously. Patanjali has pointed out four kinds of sleep, closely related to the *gunas*:

1. Dull sleep in the heaviness of *tamas*, which is a kind of stupor.

2. Sleep filled with dreams and bewildering elements coming from *rajas*.

3. Sleep in which something remains alert because a quality of consciousness doesn't entirely disappear. In this kind of sleep, the being consciously seizes something issued from *sattva*. Something remains like an impression of night lit up by the moon.

4. Conscious sleep in which one touches the mystery of truth.

At the moment when consciousness fades away into sleep, a flash can be perceived that is exactly like the flash at the moment of awakening. These two flashes are of the same nature, of the same substance. It is said, symbolically, that this brightness lights up the head behind the forehead and is diffused throughout the head. It is represented by the moon which always adorns the forehead of Shiva.

Conscious sleep resembles the sleep of a mother who is sleeping beside her child. The child's sleep is heavy. The mother is resting, but nevertheless her sleep has a quality of alertness on account of the presence of the baby, whereas a part of herself enjoys a conscious sleep that is fed by the forces of life.

From the pages of *In Search of the Miraculous*, the voice of Gurdjieff resounds like a call, "Wake up!" Gurdjieff points out the way to awaken, to see the mechanicalness that keeps us in prison, to come out of the automatism of heavy matter, but he does not speak of the stage of voluntary sleep in a state of awakened consciousness, at least according to what Ouspensky tells us. From other sources, however, we are able to see the amplitude of his mastery of this plane of sleep in a state of awakened consciousness.

There is a detailed technique for attaining this "yogic sleep," which is no longer in any way mechanical and does not obey psychological laws. Nor has it anything to do with the natural sleep of a healthy man. That is why one of the first questions a Guru asks his disciple is "How do you sleep?" and his first concern is to teach him gradually to sleep without dreaming. Another question will be "How long do you sleep?" The answer is connected with the importance attached to nocturnal vigils and meditations which are an obstacle to physiological sleep, when the silent night should be a time primarily devoted to a gradual work of conscious interiorization, followed by voluntary sleep in a state of awakened consciousness. This sleep, in a body without fatigue and without tensions (except for the minimal fatigue caused by the wear and tear of time) and in a studied posture, always the same,[6] becomes the field of many experiences.

Learn how to go to sleep consciously, starting from a very sensitive waking state, for the descent into voluntary sleep in a state of awakened consciousness has a counterpart. It is the awakening in awakened consciousness, which demands a precise discipline.

If you know this state of awakened consciousness in sleep, then you have become like the silk thread of a necklace from which all the pearls have been unstrung, one by one, in a given order. The pearls can be restrung consciously, one by one in the same order, beginning with the last, in the same rhythm with which they were unstrung. A vigilant eye follows the process. While the pearls continue to be added to one another, an X period of time will pass and, as the last pearl is added, the eyes will open. Was one really asleep or not? The answer is "yes and no."

Shrî Râmakrishna often spoke about this awakened consciousness during voluntary sleep. He said, "Enter voluntary sleep starting from the heart and not from a lower center." To picture this experience, one must imagine a lamp lit in the heart. Concentrate on the heart and move progressively to the higher planes which you know. Then, when you are sure of yourself and it is possible for you to fill all the centers of your body in the same way, without suppressing your natural impulses such as desires, greediness, passion, try it. This method has been confirmed by many yogis.

---

[6] See the Buddha's posture, lying on his right side, the right arm under the head, the left foot resting on the right foot.

VII

Observation of Oneself

In observing oneself, the first thing to do is to discover whether it is the intellect, the will, or the feeling which predominates in ourselves. Even if one of the three plays the part of hero, the others nonetheless exist. To establish co-ordination between the three is a long and exacting labor. Without this co-ordination, one of these elements will develop abnormally, and neither the Master nor the pupil will then be able to do anything about it.

To discover yourself, try to put your thought aside. Try to return consciously to animal life, to what is most primitive in you; at that moment, you will know what really belongs to you. Later, another experience will be to return consciously to the life of the plant. A plant produces flowers in its own good time, without any fuss. Flowers are food for butter-flies.

In observing oneself, nothing is necessary but these voluntary "returns" which allow us to discover what is positive and negative in us. True work is to integrate fully these observations.

Gurdjieff distinguishes at the start between man Number 1, man Number 2, and man Number 3. In India, we speak of castes. One is necessarily born into one or the other caste and enters into a life full of natural movements in which all kinds of influences (samskâras) are in play. This development is entirely automatic and would remain so were it not for the shocks blindly distributed by the cosmic energy of Shakti. This energy knocks down anyone who happens to be in its way or who stands up to it. Its whim is our luck! The shocks that come from it create rebellion. These are brief moments of awakening.

Without rebellion, man would not be conscious of his reactions; he would not begin to struggle against the unknown force that defies him. Only he who responds to the attack will, when the time comes, meet a Guru, that is, a guide, a protector; but this protector, while ensuring the desired protection, may later on become the one who will consciously direct the shocks of Shakti towards his disciple.

On this subject the Tantras say that spiritual discipline must be followed with regularity, even if it involves necessary periods of intervals. In any case, sudden deviations are inevitable in order to create the elements of new life. Shocks coming from surroundings are always a stimulant, the more so if they are provoked by the Guru himself.

It is not always possible to recognize from where shocks come, for they have sometimes the same appearance and bring the same suffering. It is only through suffering that one can discover a deeply embedded root that resists the shocks.

By being born into this or that caste, a man is a slave to

men stronger than himself, just as every beast has to submit to stronger beasts. Through successive shocks from *Shakti*, man passes through successive inner births and each time all that he knows will have to be re-learned and re-evaluated on another plane. Impressions (*samskâras*) appear always in the same succession and according to the same recurrence, but the densities will be different. Heavy as lead at the start, they will little by little become as light as the fleecy matter of the clouds.

Living spirituality is too primordial to be grasped by the intellect. Philosophers try in vain to explain in words what we feel.

In his teaching, Gurdjieff touches on two important points of this extreme positivism, namely, the heart as the seat of the emotions, and sex, the repercussions of which are still deeper and more overwhelming than those of the heart. We could "be" and "do" if we were capable of uniting the pure feelings of the heart and the pure desires of sex; in this way, we would discover the very essence of man. The ordinary Christian has the idea of paradise and of hell to help him in his evolution and, between the two, morality and the precepts of charity. In this morality no one is able to give a place to the atomic bomb and the extermination camps, which, in *prakriti*, have their place. The result is a strong rejection of responsibility, although the responsibility exists, even though it does not diminish the two natural and automatic movements of *prakriti*.

The ordinary Hindu has, properly speaking, no morality but a system of evaluation comparable to a stairway, making it possible at each step to recognize new values with their own lights and shades. Good and evil are two aspects of the same thing. Certain steps are hard to climb because of the demands inherent in them, for they stem from cosmic laws.

Fortunately, the factor "time" is there to soften any too violent movement.

The misfortune would be to remain a long time on any one step of the stairway in tepid satisfaction of some state newly reached or rediscovered, for from this there follows a dullness which is like a slow death—a true sleep in complete unconsciousness.

The steps of the stairway represent man's possible evolution. If man is free from his movements, does he have the possibility of choosing their direction? His power of choice varies from his own level of consciousness, and he has to learn how to discover at his "point of departure" what are his particular conditions and possibilities. All the rest belongs to the play (lîlâ) of prakriti. If nothing resists her, if nothing stands in her way, prakriti will thoroughly enjoy herself, her role being to create and to eat her own creation, if nothing rises in self-defense.

To work in order to know one's "point of departure" means to enter into a detailed observation of oneself. In India, in daily contact with people who do not have the type of mind which analyzes all that it perceives, it is a test of strength that breaks down the armature of logic and the ability of the intelligence to create compromises. The Hindu "swallows" things; he digests them without thinking. He puts his trust in the Lord Shiva who is continually swallowing the poison of the world so that his throat is blue from it, yet without letting this disturb his divine play.[1]

It is important that he who works toward his own evolution should discover what kind of link exists between his belief, whatever it may be, and his life, as it is lived day by day. Something links the two, be it no more than a mechanical

---

[1] The gods and the demons met together to churn the ocean and extract its nectar (amrita). It appeared, but hoping for something still more precious, the gods and the devils continued to churn. Then poison appeared.

continuity. It may be that some form of meditation will some day find a place there, making use at first of ordinary coarse habits; this meditation will finally become purer. Later on, of its own accord, it will take a different form.

Lived experience is always sustained by a living paradox:

"If you search for God, you are sure not to find Him."
"If you search for power, you will never have it."

God prefers one who struggles against Him[2] to one who is lukewarm. We can develop in ourselves only what is already in our own destiny (*svadharma*). "If you have a power in yourself, you can make it grow, absolutely nothing more."

According to a popular saying, "If you worship God, He will ruin you, but if you still love Him, He will become the slave of your slave."

The *Chandi*[3] illustrates this as follows: "The demon Shumba felt the desire to possess a goddess who had come down from heaven. He said to his messenger, 'I want this woman. If she does not come to me, I shall drag her to me by the hair. Go tell her so! The messenger left and transmitted the demon's order. The goddess smiled and said to the messenger, 'I made a vow a very long time ago, before I heard of a master like yours. It was this: My husband will be none but he who insults my pride! Tell your master to come to me and ask me to marry him! I await him!'"

The great obstacle in every spiritual discipline is fear. Another obstacle, still more dangerous, is meek and passive obedience. A famous Guru said, "I am surrounded by people who do everything I wish, who obey all my requests. They are like sheep! I would rather see people work from love—

---

[2] In India, one who struggles against God . . . see p. 141.
[3] One of the oldest *Puranic* texts forming part of the *Markandeyapurâna*.

a love that sets on fire, that generates life. Naughty children are the ones who have the most possibilities in them!"

If we obey our passions—greed, anger, envy, laziness—it is because we worship them as idols well hidden in us. If we throw light on them, we cannot avoid seeing them and finding them horrible. We detest them and at the same time do not wish to be separated from them.

There is an exact science for cultivating memory; on the other hand, there is an exact science for cultivating forget-fulness.[4] The one is as important as the other. Every day I eat with pleasure, but do I save the skin of an orange from which I have extracted the juice? In the same way, the past has its importance, but one has to remember events as they come to mind without allowing feeling to enter into it. Each day a child plays with the toys that amused him the day before, but without remembering the sensations he experienced, for he does not connect one thing with another. We must consciously regain this possibility.

You must learn to welcome consciously the most unexpected events of life, to be entirely transparent in front of them, without any motive, either right or wrong. At that moment avoid all judgment, for you do not know what law is in operation.

Hold back your *prakriti* in all the spontaneous movements that arise in it, so that it does not flow out or become diverted toward the *prakriti* of others. This calls for no drawing back on your part; it allows you to prevent your heavy matter from becoming agglutinated with the disorder of other heavy matters. In this way you will be able to observe the movements and erratic nature of others and this will help you to catch sight of your own movements. At that point, control can be exercised, but only of yourself.

4 See p. 182.

This state of "transparency" has a relation to what you can also call "self-remembering," if you clearly understand that *prakriti* includes the entire being in the multitude of its conscious and unconscious manifestations.

Only little by little does one become used to the idea of the Void.

The best way to approach it is to do nothing from one's own initiative, but simply to watch how things are being done. What we call "our" will is not really ours. It is simply an upsurge of the vast *prakriti* in us, an automatic movement.

It must not be forgotten that if the bud has come, the full bloom is sure to follow quite naturally. Then why be in haste? All true creation begins in silence. Unfold yourself, or rather let Great Nature unfold herself in you. Blossoming will follow a logical development. Our only duty is to return to ourselves and at the same time to be alert.

The following paradox is revealing: One must hold tightly onto the rudder of the boat that symbolizes our life, be absolutely one with it, risk everything without ever letting go of the helm. At the same time, one must know that everything is temporary—the boat, the sea and ourselves.

Although holding fast, I give up everything in advance. I hold fast, noting at the same time the impermanence of everything. At that moment the play of thought ceases, there is only the "I" that knows, in the pulsation of my blood.

Do not hurry in any of your actions; be aware of exactly what dictates them. Control your thoughts before acting, which will make you slower in your actions and enable you to remain whole. You will feel an inner satisfaction if you try to have this attitude. Never make a "point-blank" decision. As women say, "Haste makes a bad curry!"

Remember everything you do, for the smallest things are

the most important. Remember everything you think. This control will be established once and for all as soon as you know how to record a fact in itself. Speak to your heart, but without using words. Learn to live in this discipline to manifest your life.

Those who transmit a teaching do so because they have decided to return towards the masses and help others approach the threshold of knowledge. But one must know that no particle of truth can be given, for we know nothing of another's thought. Never. To believe it would be to create an illusion as dangerously false as that of human love. Truth can be lived only after a very long purification.

There are several disciplines of voluntary detachment.

A traditional one is that of the adepts of *Vedanta* who, to put an end to the relation of cause and effect (*karma*), plunge into detachment by taking the solemn vows of *sannyâsa*. From that time on, their discipline is constantly to discriminate between the real and the unreal. That is why, under the ocher robe, there are so many monks who, at the beginning of their asceticism, are wicked, miserly, greedy, and liars. They are cleansing the inner being. This work is slow and painstaking. Throughout this asceticism and because of their robe, they are sustained by their surroundings, helped by the whole of a society that trusts them, by the people that ask their blessing and fear their anger.

Another traditional discipline is that in which, in everyday life, I consciously die to myself each evening, to be reborn each morning, infinitely supple, malleable. It is life in its fullness in the immediate present. "I am the thread of the necklace, the thread that holds the beads together." Each bead is an experience. In relation to its transmuted raw material, each bead is perfect in itself. Who am I, if not the whole of these transmutations? To be passed beyond, they must first be brought back to a central point.

The process of externalization of any spiritual experience must be observed with care and precision. That is where our attention must be directed for a very long time, for it will reveal how the process opposed to exteriorization operates, provided the observer knows how to see what takes place in him.

The mystery will always be that "the All" is discovered by coming back into oneself, and not through the process of exteriorization. Within oneself, there is no longer any surrender to outer will, but an immersion in the principle of a higher will. The Bâül and the Sufi know this very well. One returns from it a different being even if one cannot make the experience last. It is illuminating. That is all. Intellectually, one invents means to reach it, whereas it is rather a question of chemistry, of transformation. If you could understand that, the transformation of one element into another would passionately interest you—earth into water, water into fire, fire into air, and so forth. These words are only the keys to studying what takes place in us at different densities of being.

One of the means used is voluntary detachment. The only true detachment is a result and not an effort. It can be compared to the scales that fall by themselves from the skin of a snake; the snake does nothing; in the same way the bark of certain trees cracks and falls off when the trunk grows thicker. The same phenomenon takes place in the inner being after the digestion of an integrated experience. The experience itself disappears like a good meal. Food is distributed throughout the body according to a known process, which we shall not go into here. What applied to food applies also to living experience; if it is perfectly integrated, there is no more to be said about it. It is quickly forgotten, but the inner being has grown.

If I speak of God, it is because I do not know who God is, what God is. He who speaks about something is outside of that thing. The only truth is the radiation of the being in living silence. But it is easy to be mistaken, for in the "return" to life, he who knows is as mute as a stone. The "Great Manu" advises us to be silent. He who questions is conscious of his heavy matter, he who is silent is conscious of the transforming ferment that dwells in him.

He who, without wishing it, without even thinking about it, transforms something in the being of people around him, has a power attributed in the old days to the philosophers' stone. It is the ferment of an integrated experience. In the course of this process, the disciple must be patient and calm like a fisherman on the water's edge. The fisherman has cast his line; the disciple has opened his heart. What will appear comes from the depths of the water, from the depths of the heart. Neither one nor the other knows what it will be. To be ready is the only thing that counts. This waiting causes the disciple to die to what is around him.

There can be no question of repeating this experience. To try to repeat it would be committing a great mistake which could be fatal, for it would mean voluntarily engaging the ego in the play of powers (*siddhis*) and cosmic forces without being prepared to control them.

One or the other of the traditional Schools always offer yogic experiences: meeting and contact (*darshan*) with a saint, revelation, discipline for the mind, the heart, the body, life in an *âshram*, and so forth. All these experiences are at our disposal. They are our chance. They have been tried by others before us, and we can rely on them according to our individual type.

These experiences can fill a life. Nevertheless, they are only the careful tilling of naturally fertile ground before a single true sensation is felt within and can be incarnated. This sensation is the seed of life because it is entirely pure. It creates, then disappears. Its role is ended. The child to be born is potentially the embryo in the matrix of the inner being, which will one day be the "Man whose seat is in the cavern of the heart." There is no mystery in this. One faces reality.

If the spirit can become malleable matter and matter made supple become spirit, spiritual experience will demonstrate that it can transform the behavior of the individual. This transformation—spirit-matter and matter-spirit—is, in fact, true spiritual existentialism, the consciousness of *Sat*. But in a time of danger and depression, when the passions reign which characterize the vital plane, the human hunger—represented in the West by "existentialism"—distorts the view of "pure Existence" (*Sat*).

In every spiritual discipline thought goes ahead, words come after. The body follows only very slowly. Only then can one speak of total surrender. To establish a discipline that engages all the functions of the body is long and difficult because the body is heavy and asleep (*tamas*). In the life of the world, the body is made use of first. It is educated and given all kinds of habits until its behavior is considered satisfactory.

Most people ignore everything connected with the internal sense organs (*indryas*). The internal organ of thought has nothing in common with habitual thoughts turned toward the outside. It is used very rarely. The internal organ of speech is still more rarely used. Interiorized life only uses the internal sense organs, which have a double function, that of relating us to outer life and of bringing to us impressions to be stored. To recognize the functioning of these inner organs (*indryas*) means very careful work on oneself.

Certain laws must not be revealed before a long preparation has given them weight. Only in direct experience will their substance come alive and their existence be demonstrated. These laws are part of the interiorized experience, of the substance of life that has been "sucked" from the Void; it can be neither eaten nor drunk, it can only be absorbed into oneself.

Here are some fragments of it. It is said, "Take a broom and sweep before you." On the philosophical plane, this means "to separate oneself from *prakriti*." Part of oneself is passive and remains calm and unmoved; the other part of oneself is active, in movement, constantly in action and re-action.

We see a dog chained to his kennel. The dog is barking, but he does not know that he is barking. He is only fulfilling the function for which he is there. Animals have consciousness, but not self-consciousness. The heart of the problem that interests us is the following: "Have an eye open on yourself, observe yourself!" In life you are, in fact, like the barking watchdog; you are always watching *others*, but you never look at yourself with the same keenness.

Another way to formulate this idea is the following: One man smokes opium, relishing his experience; another smokes without being intoxicated because he measures what he does. Still another remains indifferent while he smokes. He feels nothing because he functions like an automaton. He is the image of sleep in the waking state where there are no reactions. These different planes form the major part of the teaching of Gurdjieff, as it has been reported by Ouspensky. They have been given exactly. But in his own teaching, Gurdjieff touched on many other planes as well.

In your efforts of self-observation you are regularly stopped at the precise point where you are unable to concretize what to you appears as objective. If you knew how to do it, you would know what "pure joy" (*Ânanda*) is. But as yet you have only a few rare memories of those moments which, although vivid, soon disappear. To taste this joy in the essence of the being would make you independent. At that point one is virtually separated from *prakriti*. That is why intoxication is the oldest form of worship, a bliss of remembrance no longer bound by time. Orthodox Hindu widows are perfectly familiar with this state. They reach these pure delights through the rigorous asceticism of their life.

One must know how to pass consciously to the plane of pure sensation. To get there, one must learn to orient oneself between two kinds of memory (*smritis*): memory of an event and memory of the essence that has been recognized. One of these memories is changeable, the other permanent. Memories of the event exist only in time. As long as they remain in time, one is happy or distressed, according to the nature of the memories. As soon as a sensation is associated with them, they become a limitation, that is to say, "what is finished" or "what is lost."

A pure memory is never a sensation, but the delight of having touched a "point." Hence the importance of pure things: what lies around us, what we hear and see, what we eat and breathe. Only pure memories lead to eternal memory in which the impressions of life (*samskâras*) are effaced. One touches here a state of deep spiritual existentialism which is the "eternal present." But every time one speaks about it, one destroys something of the power that is in play, for instead of interiorizing it, one exteriorizes it. That is why a Master who has accepted the task of teaching is sacrificing himself. He acts according to a descending law. The "substance" of the experience that he makes possible for others to approach is like the fetus in a pregnant woman. The Master follows the experience without imagining the form that it will take. He loves the "child" before it has name and form (*nama-rupa*).

The greatest mistake we can make is to believe that we can direct our actions, whereas all we can do is to feel the repercussions and reactions to which they give rise. One attitude, however, is possible, namely, that of forgetting the action as and when it is in progress. The result will be a blank page in which memories will no longer leave an imprint.

A Buddhist discipline suggests, "Do not attach the moment that is passing to another moment." Of what use is it to connect one to the other? Live like the child holding a toy in his hand. He gives it with a smile to one person and refuses it to another.

If one studies the life of Shankarâchârya in his mystical period, one sees that a great saint never acts according to his own will, but according to the will of others, who may be madmen. This means to act without creating inner reaction. In this state of freedom, the creative impulse arises. You will serve better, you will participate in the life of others, and you will be able to laugh heartily at yourself!

There exists a philosophy of forgetting; practice it! The Nyâya School teaches, "From a lower *prakriti*, aspire to reach a higher *prakriti*. To get there, free yourself from past relationships; throw away your memories, which weigh so heavily. When sustained by *prakriti*, your memories are stale food. Throw them in the Ganges, which has a strong current, but not into a pond, where they would decay without being destroyed."

In the way of love (*bhakti*), observation of oneself remains fully conscious of the recurrent movements of human nature even when they are violent; but observation of oneself is freed in the stage of interiorization where the essence of being is only nourished by very subtle foods (*prânâ*). In this new state of consciousness, there is no longer any suffering arising from *prakriti* because the clear consciousness is now inhabited only by the spirit (*Purusha*). As proof, we have near us the example of Sârada Devî, who used all the movements of *prakriti* whatever they were, but kept them outside her "being of purity," which was nourished from another source.

For the woman, who is consciously a manifested form of the spirit (*Purusha*), giving birth to the divine-infant (Gopala)[5] becomes a subtle reality with each passage from one state of consciousness to another. Each passage is marked by the deep night of a total sacrifice. There are successive births accompanied by deeper and deeper pains. This mystical childbirth is a reality in the mental as in the physical realm. Man remains a stranger to this process of childbirth. That is why, in every age, "virgins" have given birth to beings of light, to divine incarnations.

Observation of oneself can only be directed by a Master who knows his disciple and will help him to see his problems. The work of interiorization is perfectly codified by Patanjalî, who in his aphorisms gives a detailed plan of work. But this detailed discipline remains up to the Master who knows his student's type and sees his possibilities of development.

Patanjalî specifies the following states:

1. A personal discipline to quiet the body.

2. A state of consciousness in which calm has been established, but the subconscious continues to work.

3. The mastery of tendencies and habits that reappear one after the other at long intervals.

4. A taste of freedom that can be called illumination, even if it is partial and ephemeral, when a tendency or habit is overcome.

Follow these simple and sure rules of conduct. Be silent as to your results and pass on crumbs of knowledge only to those nourished by the same blood as you, who are not prone to bitter criticisms and fault finding. Avoid those who pride themselves on their strength, for it serves only *prakriti*. You

[5] The name given to the Child-Krishna who plays with the shepherds.

are never obliged to participate in the life of someone who is not one of your co-disciples or a spiritual son of your Guru.

With the Master, be simple. Learn to have integrity. Serve him without asking questions, completely surrendered, but without any emotion.

Patanjalî gives the psychological foundations[6] resulting from the experience of centuries and suggests two formulas:

1. Relax all the joints, which activates inner suppleness. There is a feeling of being at one with the earth. From this comes the deep physical joy of having a harmonious body.

2. Only with a global sensation of the whole body can one begin to observe the breath, which goes outwards, whereas it is in fact the inner life.

If we try to observe in this way, without giving rise to the least tension or alteration, whether in thought, or in feeling, or in the body, it is possible to follow the movement of the breath and to isolate oneself in the body as in an impregnable citadel. Seat yourself in a natural way. This will be your ideal posture (âsana). Observe your breathing while allowing it to establish its own rhythm. Discover calmly whether this rhythm is introverted or extroverted, that is, whether you naturally hold your breath inside or whether the breath stops for a moment after breathing out. Then breathe normally through both nostrils. To begin with, the breath has no rhythm. Later a rhythm settles down, provided one does not interfere.

In the beginning, the breathing is only physical, but little by little, as the rhythm deepens, it will go down to the center of gravity of the body and will cause it to vibrate internally. There is a saying, "The mind is the Master of the activities of the senses, but the breathing is the ruler of the mind."

---

[6] See *Commentaries on the Aphorisms of Patanjalî (Râja-Yoga)*.

VIII.

Automatism

The law of automatism is absolute. Since its role is to keep the masses bound to the will of *prakriti*, it forces the man who is a seeker or disciple by nature to find a way out and awaken to his own being.

To succeed in this several things are required:

1. An active meditative state in all the circumstances of life, that is, to become the witness of oneself in the very midst of life.

2. A voluntary withdrawal from all the mental functions—in which by association of ideas the majority of reactions arise.

3. Silencing all greed in oneself.

In India women reach this awakening through "natural intelligence," that is, through their essence, whereas a man can reach it only through voluntary sacrifice and personal discipline. There is no other way for him.

It is acknowledged that a hundred thousand seekers will be reduced to nothing for the sake of one who reaches the goal, just as in nature an immense surplus of seeds is required for one to bear fruit. All the wasted seeds go to make good humus for the earth. The spiritual atmosphere of India is composed of all the disciples who follow a spiritual discipline and also those who come to nothing. Hindus do not discuss their attempts nor complain of their failures in this domain. For them all movements coming from the ego are equally worthless; all of them spring from wrong impulses. Hence every good action performed of one's own initiative still belongs to the realm of personality.

Ideas and sensations are as automatic as everything else. They can be counted and classified, their frequency can be recognized. They are only figures and lines forming triangles with unequal sides.[1] One has to know this rhythm of life.

This leads to the study of auditory sensation which is at the origin of the scale. The intervals with their various frequencies of vibration determine the notes and not the notes that determine the intervals. The same succession of irregular intervals occurs in everything manifested. Brahmâ himself creates in accordance with a rhythm that has its own vibration.

Life rolls on and carries much offal along with the stream. We need not haul it ashore but let it float on and disappear.

To appreciate rightly Shrî Râmakrishna's vision of infinity in his childhood on seeing white cranes flying through the sky, or the ecstatic force that drove Shrî Râmana Maharshi to the Void, one has to feel very deeply in oneself the continuous pressure that Hindu society can exert on a delicate being, and the spell gradually cast upon him by the attitude of the family, the village, the caste from which there is no way out.

[1] See p. 131.

These extremely rigid conditions cause beings ready to throw off the yoke to "explode," just as the pressure of the earth causes one seed in a thousand to burst open. Each tree, indeed, is a miracle of persistent effort to survive in the midst of multiple dangers. This effort is a movement of the essence, still incoherent but already prepared to pay the price of independence.

Do not leave your soul in the hands of the temple priests, but become your own architect and lay the foundations of a solid structure in which everything will be in its place. It is by progressively studying our reactions to shocks from outside that we can see our progress and what remains shaky in ourselves.

The only way to recognize your real "I" is to see your reactions in detail, one after the other. That is the surest guide on the way to inner being. The duration of a reaction is the only moment when mind and matter, soul and body are not cut off from each other. It is a moment of your own reality.

If we knew how to expand into the infinite in time and space, nothing would be difficult and the complexities of life would disappear. They would be carried by life itself, in other words the "Divine Mother," or the "Void" in which Life is creative, the first cause of *prakriti*.

India lives on this idea. Each one individually does what he can on his own level of understanding. This idea is the generator of all upward flight as of all degradation.

India also believes in successive births. This belief is acknowledged and repeated to the point where it is devoid of thought and meaning. He who lives with consciousness not yet awakened will be reborn on the same plane of evolution, as the tree, on its plane, is reborn as a tree. It is matter and remains matter in the admirably organized recurrence of *prakriti*.

The man who penetrates willingly into the plane of evolution, creates impressions (*samskâras*) related to it which by accumulating bring him under the evolutionary will. There ensues a definite rhythm of births and deaths (*samsaras*) until substances in him are refined and purified. The level of consciousness changes at each stage, for many degrees of perception mark out the path of evolution. New words come to be used from the language of alchemy and physics, for it is easier to observe a scientific event than an inner attitude in which subjectivity is involved and therefore spoils every objective observation.

Gurdjieff clearly refers to Buddhist disciplines when he says, "Be conscious of each of your movements," and when he describes in detail the mechanism of automatism to which we are subjected. By being conscious of oneself it is possible to pass from the plane of personality to the plane of essence, for an observer is then present. The *Upanishads* and the *Bhagavad Gîtâ* indicate different means, each one representing fragments of discipline:

1. To observe oneself with a sustained look.

2. To stand aside without any kind of judgment whatsoever, thus allowing the essence to grow.

3. A neutral look will automatically see the disorder that reigns in the inner house; a desire for order will arise of itself.

4. A growing essence always assents.

5. The essence will become "the one that carries everything in its arms," and *prakriti* will follow obediently, and finally find its own place in all the functions.

6. In the end the Lord in the heart always conquers *prakriti*.

IX

Consciousness

Even the adepts of *Sâmkhya* discuss the origin of consciousness just as much as do the philosophers, Buddhists, Vedantists, and others.

Truth is a mystery like life itself. It can be felt, it can be lived, but it cannot be analyzed and put into words. All experiences gradually move from outside inwards in order to become assimilated with the primal life which is our "essence." Then someday they find expression in their own way by radiation. This radiation is also automatic.

To be one's own self, that is to say, to live in the consciousness of one's own essence, promotes growth of a new understanding. It is just as if delicate fingers were opening the petals of a lotus of light one after another.

Between the spasmodic movements of the finite and the immobility of the Infinite a continuous stream of *Shakti* flows.

This is the process of becoming. It can be said that the force of *Shakti* is continuous as she appears to consciousness, but if you call her unconscious, then its movement will appear to be in jerks, from point to point, and things will have a beginning and an end.

But consciousness, even at the mental level, aims at continuity. It lives by duration. And duration is not a blank word. This idea is at the root of the Vedic conception of reality as pure Existence (*satyam*), Time rhythm (*ritam*), and ever growing (*brihat*). The last is the link between the first two. This is the fundamental law of spiritual evolution.

Between two different levels in a being in search of himself there is always an empty space to be crossed which provokes a chaotic movement; the more protracted the effort to cross the gap, the more violent the movement becomes.

The intermediate consciousness which opens up the way to pass from one center to another is of a very fluid "matter." It is in the heart of this matter that the Guru drives his plowshare. This fluid matter has a connection neither with the subject nor with the object—it will find its own form in the Void. It can be activated only by the Master. For a long time, the seeker himself knows nothing about it. He has no "organ" with which to discover it or make use of it.

In this situation, the disciple's attitude is to do nothing of his own will, for everything would be distorted. But he must observe clearly, on his level of understanding, all that takes place, and learn to recognize that "active passivity" that will become a right movement when the time comes. This is all that concerns him.

On the subject of the states through which Shrî Râmakrishna passed in order to return to a normal state of consciousness after a long period of *samâdhi*, he said of himself, "Since the ego never dies, let it at least become a good servant of the Divine Mother!" To come out of ecstasy, when he still felt impelled to go further away, he used to strike himself violently on the head. He said, "One can sing an ascending scale: *sa, ri, ga, ma, pa, dha, ni,* but one cannot hold the last note for long. One has to come down again!" He had an intense wish to live, to have the whole universe enter into the field of his experience. He saw life whole, complete in *Shakti,* the life of the cosmic laws, and he absorbed it to the very limit.

Every disciple in his quest is aware that the personal discipline he accepts has a practical aim, which is the union of human consciousness with the highest reality. The aim is to reach the understanding of the ultimate reality (Shiva-*Shakti*) by transforming the mental, vital, and even the physical nature of his being, even to the smallest cells in the body.

The extreme relativity of consciousness must never be forgotten. Those who have a highly developed personality are less able to be penetrated by a new form of consciousness.

Every morning wake up as a little child. At noon, stand majestically before the world, a full-bodied woman. In the evening, be a conscious being ripened in strength and serenity, who, having drunk deep at the fountain of life, now wishes to see its other face in death. In the depths of the night, be the Void itself, the darkness of the sky in which the moon shines brilliantly.

In this picture, I am giving you the secret of the *Gayarti*[1] of the *Vedas,* the essence of the Sun and the law of Life.

[1] The invocation which is pronounced every morning.

X

Sensations

All spiritual experiences are sensations in the body. They are simply a graded series of sensations, beginning with the solidity of a clod of earth and passing gradually, in full consciousness, through liquidness and the emanation of heat to that of a total vibration before reaching the Void. The road to be traveled is long.

Each time a step is made on the ascending ladder, a sensation of expansion in space and of complete relaxation is experienced. This sensation offers a foretaste of what the experience of pure Spirit (*Chit*) might be, in which all things are transcended. How far one is from that! Yet at this moment spirit and matter appear to be one. This conception comes from an ancient theory of the purification of the elements which in the *Tantras* is called *bhuta-shuddhi*.

May your present discipline become for you this subtle

gradation of sensations, a means for expansion and later for infiltration into everything around you, both beings and things. Become aware of the deep and strong sensation of passing from one element to another. There is no other means. Make use for this purpose of the solitude that makes it possible to interiorize many forces. Every contraction generates heat and heat expands. True personal discipline (*tapasya*) is nothing but this expansion of one's being radiating warmth produced by inner concentration.

Always remember that any sensation of expansion you may experience is a radiation. Remain calm and radiate this warmth. Do not question. Ask for nothing more. Live these moments to the full. This radiation is in itself *Shakti*, an instant of living consciousness, that is, a direct experience that is ingrained in you. Your sensation is the proof of it, a certainty you cannot efface from your memory.

In meditation, the whole body is utilized to discover a sensation of expansion which, for a long time, represents the final aim. Work on the body is a delicate attempt and has to be done according to very precise data, for each movement, voluntary or involuntary, is a search for stillness, that is to say, for a sensation of physical consciousness.

The first objective to reach is perfect solidity of the motionless body. To arrive at that, all thoughts have to be brought back one after another to the body—to its form, its weight, its balance. There must be no other thought. This state is symbolized by the matter "earth," in the heart of which, notwithstanding its heaviness and opacity, a vibration exists.

The attention will gradually be turned to the image of a vessel. The body is really that vessel made of heavy matter. It contains an effervescent wine. Concentrated on itself, attention will enter into the body, go down the length of the spinal column until there is an impression of a heaviness in the center of gravity. The whole body has then become as hard as a statue with a pure form.[1]

At that point, all the movements inside the vessel are perceptible: effervescence, agitation, ideas, images—all of them produced by the body. The stability of the body is a state in itself. This is why so much importance is attached to food and hygiene.

The second stage begins when the body, in its well-established solidity, can become the matrix of energy in movement. Externally hard, the body internally becomes the pulsation of life that fills it. An intense vibration of energy throbs in it. This state is symbolized by purification of the element water, that is to say, by the transition from a heavier to a lighter density.

Then comes the discovery that a body of radiant and very subtle sensations is contained within the body of flesh. It is only when the body of flesh has a solid form that the nerve channels (nadis) can be perceived with all the sensations of the currents of life through them. As it is said in the Vedas, "A stream flows through a rock."

The third stage is when all the currents of nervous energy flowing through the inner body become currents of light from which little by little a sensation of fire emanates. This state is symbolized by the purification of the element fire, so much so that the temperature of the body rises as in an attack of fever.

These three stages—that of solidity of the body, of sensation of the nervous currents, of the sensation of currents of light—are characteristics of meditation in depth. Up to this point, the individuality remains intact, expressed by the words, "one of the many."

The fourth stage is that in which individuality is lost. The state of sensation of fire which consumes the body is a further

[1] Vâlmîki, while in this state of solidity of the body, is said to have been covered with white ants.

transition from a heavier to a more subtle density. The fire that consumes the inner body consumes at the same time all sense of form, to the degree that the sensation of non-form becomes irradiant. This state is symbolized by the purification of the element air. The habitual impulse to resort to forms disappears. There remains only the Void, which is at the same time a precise and global sensation of multiformity. All is clarity and calm.

Meditation is in fact a laboratory work and an attack against *prakriti* to escape from her slavery.

There are different spiritual densities owing to which the "inner being" can become fluid and discover what is beyond the form of his habitual being. He can thus come in contact with beings belonging to the densities discovered. Any emotion whatsoever interrupts this process. Emotion is always an identification that prevents any movement of expansion in breadth and any movement of interiorization in depth. It blocks one of the most subtle aspects of knowledge, the passage from one density to another.

It is true that the yogis of certain disciplines are able to feed at a distance on the fluid bodies of things existing elsewhere or to find nourishment from the air. This is no miracle; it is simply a question of expansion and of the capacity to assimilate one or another kind of food.

From this point of view, conscious death is no more than the passage from one density to another, in full consciousness of the inner being. In *prakriti* there are many degrees and levels of expansion. God, the Creator, and the soul, while being the very finest parts of *prakriti*, are nevertheless materialities, even if they are fluid. A human being has infinite possibilities of expansion; he can even approach the objective Will, which is a quite different order from that of the ordinary will. The objective Will can be ascertained and felt as though a hand strikes you in the face.

Those who work on themselves generally proceed by intermittent leaps after having received shocks from life that have awakened them, or after having been in grave danger.

In a moment of inner calmness, one can gradually, as if coming out of a dream, learn to catch the last impression received and observe it without losing it. The effort to try is to isolate the sensation provoked by an impression and trace it back to the center where it arose. One sees that which provoked it. In this attempt, the slightest discussion with oneself, or the slightest fear, curiosity, or judgment, will instantly put an end to the effort.

This observation can be verified in morning dreams. A useful attempt is to wake up without shocks and to follow the indications just given, aware that the whole being never dreams. One center at a time is exteriorized in dreams; usually it is the emotional center. Only those in whom consciousness is already active dream with the whole of their being, but then this dream is no longer a dream; it belongs to another state of consciousness.

To penetrate into that realm of consciousness, sensation is the only guide we have—a continuous sensation which, even if it almost disappears or if it stays with us in a subtle way, can no longer be felt in our body. This sensation is nevertheless connected with inner organs of perception whose role and use are not yet known to us.

How to keep this sensation of oneself alive during sleep? The first effort to try is to go to sleep consciously, remaining aware of a subtle sensation of the self. This sensation will persist far beyond the ordinary state of consciousness which falls into the heaviness of sleep. This subtle sensation becomes a vibration of life through a process that is precisely known. On waking, the reverse process takes place. To animate the sensation of the self the vibration of life will unfold itself long before the body awakens.

How to connect these two moments of sensation of the self, separated by the sleep of the body? In this realm nothing can be willed. The progressive refining of the heavy matters in us will allow us to discover, one after another, the inner organs (*indryas*) of perception.

When we try to control to some extent the impressions coming to us from outside and the sensations they create in us, it is important not to allow more than one sensation at a time to pervade us—one that is identifiable. We may then be able to detect its color, its taste, smell and sound, and finally a certain tangibility in it. At that moment, we shall know exactly where it comes from and how to evaluate it.

The co-existence of several sensations gives rise to comparisons, judgment, interest, and attachment—hence, inevitably, causes a confusion.

We can ask the question, "Why do I exist?" One of the customary answers is that we exist because of the law of cause and effect (*karma*). One can voluntarily ignore the idea of *karma*, in spite of all the philosophical explanations given about the relation of cause to effect coming from former lives and influencing future lives. But what cannot be ignored are the various categories of impressions (*samskâras*), the shocks coming from outside which are constantly hitting us. We live on these impressions as on the air we breathe and the food we absorb. We must learn to recognize these impressions, to welcome them or to reject them. An exact science is involved here, in which the influence of the father, of the mother, and of the Guru is of the highest importance.

To learn to discriminate as objectively as possible entails an all-round work of the whole being in which nothing is left in the dark. At that moment one knows why one lives, one discovers the meaning of Life within life, one's own place in the harmony of a great law. Each conquest is a sign of peace and enlightenment on one's own level of consciousness until that level is surpassed. No haste. The conscientious seeker goes from deep obscurity to a lesser obscurity. He speaks by negations, but these negations are positive. If the road is long, great patience is required.

What is a true spiritual discipline? It is a known rhythm of the harmonized body. All is there. Nothing could be more material than to use the body for acquiring a right sensation of God. Hence the many customs regulating relationships between people, caste taboos, and so forth to prepare for the harmonious union of an awakened body with consciousness and with the eternal *prakriti*. Through spiritual discipline the entire body becomes the receptacle of divine sensations. A well-conducted discipline makes it possible to identify and recognize at its base a unique sensation which is a sensation of the universe. What is known meditation is the interiorization of this "pure sensation" outside of time. It is a taste of eternity.

Discipline, that is to say, voluntary sacrifice, is the unique means to reverse the direction of the vital current which is habitually directed outwards by the mind. From this comes the image of the disciple going against the current of vital fluid to make his way up to the source, just as, on the concrete plane, thousands of pilgrims go to the Ganges upstream to its source.

As a matter of fact, I am contradicting myself when I speak to you of discipline, for I make a point always that every one of you emphasizes and intensifies his own motive for search. The whole thing is to have a very definite motive as the pivot around which your attempt will be organized. People often come to me and say, "I would like to meditate on something, for example, a flame, a triangle, a luminous spot. What do you advise?" In this case I answer, "Well then, meditate on your body. Try to find a right sensation of yourself!"

A right sensation of oneself is in the very nature of incarnation, of penetration. At that moment, the spirit becomes matter and takes on a definite density in the body. Personal austerity (*tapasya*) is the process by which a sensation comes alive, so that the whole body glows. This is a true sensation, that of spirit becoming flesh.

This state in which no thought enters is experienced as an intense bodily bliss (*Ânanda*), for in the state of awakened consciousness it is precisely felt as a global sensation, a wholeness. We are here touching the hidden secret of Buddhism.

The experience of a pure sensation in the physical body is in the realm of the nerve channels (*nadis*) which allow the vibrations perceived, namely, extremely fine substances, to penetrate into the physical body.

This leads to the realm of music—notes and intervals. Between notes there are intervals of varying lengths, the particularities of which are known. Make the following experiment: concentrate on any one musical note and feel in yourself the modulation and the length of its vibrations. The low notes resound at the base of the spinal column, the middle ones in the region of the heart, the high notes in the head.

Although the rhythm and notation of the *Sâmaveda* have been lost, the notion has survived that the human organism as a whole represents different levels of consciousness obeying the same laws of modulation and frequency of sound. Each note is in itself a pure sound (*nâdâ*) and pure Bliss (*Ânanda*) with different vibrations. There are eight circuits of nerves (*nadis*) along the spinal column. The vibrations vary according to the movement of the sun. For that reason there are special chants for the short moment immediately preceding the dawn (*bhairava*) and for the exact moment of dawn itself (*bhairavi*). Chaitanya[2] used to pass from one ecstasy to another when hearing the name of God sung. One of his companions who was always with him composed some well-known melodies based on his lamentations and pleadings with the Divine.

An orthodox swâmi, going through a village, paused in front of a poor mud house. Somebody was laughing, somebody was singing. Intrigued, the swâmi went nearer and held out his bowl. He saw a woman feeding her children. There were five of them sitting on the ground—four beautiful children, and a fifth. To his great surprise, the fifth was the Child-Krishna, a statuette made of wood and plaster such as are sold in the markets. The mother was making a little ball of rice and putting it into one mouth after another. The Child-Krishna was receiving his share and this was why they were all laughing.

"What are you doing?" cried the swâmi. "How do you dare to play with the Lord Krishna and offer him that unclean food which goes from mouth to mouth? What sacrilege!" Frightened, the woman prostrated herself at the monk's feet. "My lord swâmi," she said, "I had no idea I was doing wrong. My children are so happy to play with Shrî Krishna. He is their companion. If I have offended the Supreme, how can I be pardoned? Please help me!"

"Give me that statuette," said the monk severely, "and I will take it to the village temple where the Lord Krishna will be bathed and worshiped rightly and treated with respect instead of being used as a plaything. You will visit him when bringing your offerings to the priests!"

The children were upset. They were losing their friend.

---

[2] A celebrated reformer and monk in Bengal (1485–1527). He himself was neither a poet nor a musician, but he inspired his disciples in such a way that over three centuries thousands of devotional songs were composed in Bengal.

The mother wept for shame. She wrapped the statuette and
gave it to the swâmi. He carried it to the temple and told the
priests what he had seen. They were outraged. But the same
night the swâmi could not go to sleep. Suddenly the Lord
Krishna appeared to him in all his glory. "What have you
done?" he said to the monk. "I was so happy at that woman's
house! I loved her devotion and her laughter, and now you
have shut me up in a dark temple. Listen, I will not eat anything nor accept any offerings until you take me back to her.
Her rice was cooked just right and that is the rice I want—no
other!"

Sacred images (*mûrti*) of gods and goddesses have two
aspects. The first is the philosophical aspect of a principle, the
projection of an idea (*tattva mûrti*). By this devotion, the
devotee is supposed to go beyond the image and the symbol
it expresses and discover the second aspect, which is the sensation arising from the principle that gives life to the image
(*bhâva mûrti*). This sensation is the passage from the principle to its realization in life.

A Hindu will say, "What does it mean to me, the idea of
an Absolute, of the inconceivable Brahman?[3] I do not want
to worship a reflection of light. What I want is to contemplate
the Divine and worship him in my own way. It is not the impersonal Lord Krishna in his sublime glory who fills my heart,
but rather Krishna the Child who steals butter, plays the flute,
and plays all sorts of tricks."

In this way the majestic attributes of the *tattva mûrti* are
transformed into naïve simplicity to feed a true sentiment of
the heart. The culmination of every spiritual discipline is this
precise sensation in oneself of divine love. To know how to
make use of the force and grandeur of philosophy, but in the
heart to know how to feed oneself on the radiant beauty alone.

[3] The Absolute, the impersonal God.

XI

Emotions

An absolute rule in *Sâmkhya* is never to speak about emotions. To display sorrow is only to provoke an expansion of *prakriti* instead of looking for a way towards a more fluid sensation, of going willingly towards a possible transformation of the emotion.

Here are three practical rules which, when they work together, are the basis of a state in which emotion loses its destructive power:

1. Keep yourself free of things. This creates a surface freedom.

2. Hope for nothing in the future. This gives consistency to the present and creates a freedom in time.

3. Die consciously every evening, which means a rebirth on awaking and inner freedom.

For life to become objective, there are two fundamental attitudes, namely:

1. A concentration of consciousness around the axis of the higher Will. This involves an attentive awareness of the whole being, including all its movements and functions.

2. In front of *prakriti*, adopt consciously the attitude of a child. This attitude dissolves obstacles. Even a tigress softens in front of her cub, whether it is strong or weak, good or bad. This child, whom nothing can frighten, is renewed by himself through elemental impressions—earth, water, fire, air, the beauty of a face, the intonation of a voice, a look.

As long as "my" *prakriti* does not grasp these two ways of becoming objective in the midst of the great *prakriti*, there will always be all sorts of reactions: crystallizations, breakdowns, ossifications, or other forms of psychic suffering.

All conscious work coming from within is a direct attack on the power of "my" *prakriti* and on the power of the great *prakriti*. An arithmetic progression connects the two. The greater the inner effort, the stronger "my" *prakriti*'s defense of itself becomes, the bigger the obstacles set up by the great *prakriti*. In the *Bhagavad Gîtâ*, Krishna says on the battlefield, "I will tell you a secret, do not repeat it. If you speak, you will be stoned."

Emotions constantly cause one to mistake the path for the aim and vice versa. And they are not the same! If you want to climb to the top of a mountain, do not lose yourself in sentimental ramblings about its beauty. It is better to look for a clearly marked path that will take you to the top from the spot where you are standing.

If one does not set value, positive or negative, upon emotions, one is aware of a motor that uses *prakriti* only at its habitual speed. Water in a test tube is a mass of heavy matter. As steam, the same mass of matter, while taking up more space, is also more aerated. In the same way, a human being has the capacity to transform the density of certain matters. For example, he can suffer from emotions as heavy as stone in his heart, or from emotions that have become more subtle and that, although they still exist, allow light to show through.

To "understand," whether by sustained attention or by self-observation, puts an end to the process of thinking about oneself, that is to say, it kills emotion. What remains beyond emotion must be observed with the greatest care, for the purity towards which one is tending is a state difficult to describe. It is the state of pure Existence (*Sat*).

It is unthinkable that a teacher should be impatient, for he knows that there will never be any change in *prakriti*, whether it happens to be rigid or pliable, even if one is vigilant, even if one is observing oneself. But by sustained attention anyone can touch, taste a state that is the Absolute. Alas, this "anyone," according to the *Bhagavad Gîtâ*, means *one* in a million!

Psychoanalysis works on the intensive exposure of emotions. They are brought out into the daylight with the object of cleaning out the subconscious, and thus are lived over again, which means that each of them is amplified. Instead of belonging only to the damaged part of the being, they invade the whole field of *prakriti* as the tares spread over a wheatfield.

The very structure of emotion must be denied as such, for it arises only from one's subjective view of external elements. Gurdjieff, closely following the traditional technique of Buddhist analysis, denies the existence of a negative part in the center where emotion arises, whereas he does recognize a negative part in the moving center. For this reason he tells his pupils to control negative emotions. In this way he methodically builds up one of the essential bases of inner balance by using for this purpose whatever is already partly disengaged from the heavy sleep of *prakriti*. This sleep, with its weight of ignorance, is the admirably organized automatism of Great Nature.

The traditional techniques pay no attention to emotion. Even the *Vaishnavites*, who worship Krishna and make full use of emotion in their fundamental attitude of adoration, use only those sublimated elements of emotion that sustain the ideal.

Several levels have to be passed through before one can know how to minimize emotion at its very source, to know it, to isolate and master it, and finally to be able to get rid of it. The lower stage is to realize once and for all that emotions are a debt to be paid; this realization is the beginning of a process that uproots them. This is the process of eradication. The second stage is to conceive of emotion as a surrender, an always recurring pattern. It is part of the automatism which becomes evident and really does not exist. The third stage is that in which a "light form" of an ideal is methodically and voluntarily put in the place of the "heavy form" of an emotion which is oppressive.

There are many classical examples of circles around a Master with disciples who know only the "heavy form" of an emotion and therefore interpret on their own level how the Master lives. For instance, Shrî Râmakrishna said one day, "Where is God? He is there!" and he pointed to his breast. Shrî Râmakrishna spoke from the deepest interiorization, but his disciples in their discipline were at the stage of the "heavy form" and promptly deified the man who was speaking to them. Nevertheless, they faithfully reported the intellectual part of the process.

These three stages in regard to emotion are admirably illustrated by the story of the "madwoman of Calcutta." About twenty years ago in a residential section of the city, people used to see a beautiful young woman stopping passers-by on the sidewalk in front of her house and asking them, "Where is Shyam Babu? Have you seen him? If you tell me where he is, I will go and fetch him." Her husband was dead and she was still waiting for him, kept alive by her love. And love had betrayed her. The passers-by played cruel tricks on her.

Then another phase began. She clung to young men as they were going by and said to them, "You are my Shyam Babu, you have come back. . . ." Since she was not a prostitute, these men drove her away and ill-treated her, even threw stones at her.

Several years passed and then one of her neighbors who had known her in the past noticed her sitting all day long at the foot of the sacred tree of that district. She had aged, but her face was radiant with joy. She recognized her neighbor. He asked her, "Have you found your Shyam?" "Yes," she replied with a lovely smile. "Look, there he is. . . ." and she pointed to her breast.

Renunciation (*vairâgya*) is the voluntary giving up of all emotions whatsoever. This notion, supported by a long tradition, goes hand in hand with life. This is what Gurdjieff tries to indicate and to reconcile with Christian tradition where there is nothing to support this attempt. To be capable of mastering an emotion, one has first to evaluate it and dispose of it for what it really is—the distortion of an uncontrolled and misplaced sensation.

When the intestines are out of order, one follows a strict diet. The cure comes about by abstaining for the time being from certain foods. Thus the body regains strength. Psychically, power is gathered. This method is the exact opposite of psychoanalysis, which digs about in the ego. *Sâmkhya* places you under a cosmic force and disregards the ego, saying, "Why are you afraid of this or that? All these things are only movements of *prakriti,* aspects of the eternal recurrences in men, animals, the whole of nature." One must learn to live in the very movement that shapes and molds *prakriti,* without trying to escape from it. To look at *prakriti* and see her agitated movement makes it possible not to identify with her. I observe what she is. By doing that, I feel the movement in myself, but I do not linger on the fact that I was created from the same matter. Time plays an important part in this discipline, and also patience. On the part of the Guru this patience is pure love.

Emotion does not enter into any spiritual discipline, because in itself emotion had no consistency. It is only a movement of *prakriti.* When the mind is perfectly calm it is like the still water of a mountain lake. The slightest ripple on the surface is an emotion.

What happens to it? If *Purusha* allows this ripple, however slight, to intensify and become a wave, he himself will be swallowed. Blind emotion is then master of the situation, although in fact it has no *raison d'être.*

If this emotion, while it is still only a ripple, is voluntarily interiorized, then little by little, because of its inconsistency, it will disintegrate and of itself go back whence it came.

XII

Knowledge

Knowledge, even partial, is in constant contradiction to the practical facts of daily life. Those even partly aware of this are unable to move in a straight line; they go from shock to shock in the midst of contradictions which unceasingly create reactions.

For behind every contradiction there is this irresistible something that impels us forward and that can only be approached by an extension of oneself, as a river in flood spreads its water over the land without losing sight of its bed. When I was a monk, I quarreled with *prakriti*. Monks who give up thinking become machines within the big machine of Great Nature. Kapila who transmitted *Sâmkhya* to us, showed that self-satisfaction in passive obedience can be dangerous.

To progress towards knowledge, you have wholly to live

your truth of the moment. This truth will become pure by itself by living in you. What matters most is to have an over-all feeling of the self. In this way you can see what is going on in you and know whether you are living your truth. But don't talk about it! All you can do is to irradiate this experience. It would be a mistake to speak about it.

There comes a time when a transposition must take place because a law is in question. Don't interfere; otherwise you will be taken and all the explanations you give yourself will only distort your vision. No one can bear the severity and absolute detachment of *Purusha;* that is why *prakriti* has so many intermediate truths to offer. Once you have created unity in yourself, there will be only one truth, even if it seems very far off.

Only a very few are privileged to enter the esoteric circle of knowledge, which means to put on the "armor of steel," for there the divine power is intensely active. At that time a disciple can no longer be judged by criteria of activity or non-activity. He who lives in sensation sees God in all; forms appear only to express an idea.

A time will come when two or three hundred families, each with two or three children, will live wholly in accordance with the science of inner life. The great mass of humanity will disappear or serve solely as a ground for "those who know." What will take place will again be the phenomenon of castes. The notion that castes were originally institutions of social order merely arose from ignorance. They had an esoteric meaning. In the beginning they divided people according to different modes of perception. The principles of the caste system have become atrophied and degraded in the course of inevitable deviations in the descending law. This degradation is responsible for the loss of the rules that used to regulate the passage from one state of consciousness to another. The key has been lost.

"To have eaten the mango" is an expression meaning to have tasted the fruit of knowledge. After having tasted knowledge, there is a state in which one says, "I do not know," for knowing no longer matters.

A strange fact is that one who likes discussion keeps on talking and teaching. And so much the better. On his level he is doing useful work. Vigilant observation of oneself means not to sink unconsciously into the depths that open up, but to penetrate them gradually and without shock, for the inner being has become sensitive.

It is said that the seed of knowledge has to be passed on secretly to him who is ready to receive it. After that it slowly ripens.

What becomes of those who have received this seed of Life? Some of them disappear, carrying off their treasure, and are heard of no more. But if a flame of living knowledge flares up in some definite place, the continuity of tradition will be recognized. There are well-known signs. This fact is beyond man's vision. There is no logical explanation.

Some disciples create works bearing the name of the Master from whom they have received everything with the aim of perpetuating his teaching—*âshrams*, esoteric schools, hospitals, universities and so on, which, one step lower than the Master's law, will be a way of progress for many people.

Other disciples, after a certain time, fritter away their treasure and trample it, for *prakriti* has once more enthralled them. They will seek and find a new Master, but the process of dissolution goes on without their even being aware of it because it is a part of their own nature.

In every discipline there are "those who know" and see the Divine beyond the Guru. They are exceptional, outside the ordinary ranks of man. They are the recluses who re-live the experiences of the Rishis. The priests despise them and often drive them out of their temples. But should they become famous through their asceticism and inner search, those same priests will build them temples and celebrate cults of worship and supplication in front of them (*pûjâ*).[1] "He who knows" supports the world by his realization. His only treasure is to see "That." This word represents either an abstract idea or "He who reigns in the heart of man."

Those who recognize the existence of cosmic laws through which the primordial energy expresses itself acknowledge a trinity which is: Father-Mother-Child.[2] There is a Tantric verse which says,

> True emotion
> like a pure virgin,
> dances with quick, light steps
> in the yogi's heart.

All yogis say, "This pure virgin is real emotion; it should be offered to the Lord who dwells above everything." Then the heart melts. A moment of ecstasy, of abandonment; then comes the time of return to life. Such is the power of *Shakti*. A child is conceived by this union, a child of ethereal substance. This child is a living sleep, lying twenty-four hours a day in the virgin's womb. He has been wished for.

In such a child is born in the phenomenal world, he (like all other children) is symbolically black (*tamas*-inertia) at birth. He will inevitably have to evolve and pass through the first cycle of colors which pass from black to red (*rajas*-energy). Complementary color cycles will develop from the red and pass symbolically to white (*sattva*-spirit). Amongst the complementary colors yellow is significant because it has no trace of black or red. In fact, yellow represents the energy of *Shakti*. *Shakti* herself moves in the higher knowledge of

---

[1] Shrî Râmana Maharshi (died 1950) is a striking example of this.
[2] See p. 117.

Shiva, who appears as pure white. The whiteness of Shiva radiates. Projected against the dark blue of the transcendent Krishna-*Purusha*, it appears still more luminous.

Sâmkhya says that at the time of birth on whatever plane it occurs, there is always a mixture of colors requiring purification until the white becomes pure, sparkling. He who has passed through purification becomes a Master. A Master is one who plays indifferently with all the colors of the rainbow. Black remains black, red remains red, and yellow remains yellow, each color serving some definite aim of the Master.

In the *Vedas* the three colors black (night), red (dawn), yellow (noonday sun) appear daily in the same order and disappear in the inverse order. The recurrence is rigorous. Psychologically, these three colors are the fundamental modes of expression existing in each of us. Black symbolizes the stupid heaviness or sleep of the inner being, all that which persists in the midst of the prejudices belonging to that state. Red symbolizes impetuousness and impulse, agitation, temporary subjective awakening, and sudden changes of direction. A period of agitation is always difficult but inescapable, for it is the time when *prakriti* moves by leaps and resists whatever is in front of her. This agitation will gradually cease by itself if, instead of feeding it and struggling against it, you use the force of knowledge. Yellow symbolizes a more subtle period. White is the vision of the whole in which "doing" finds its place.[3]

A Master is able at will to use the unconscious heaviness of those around him because the inertia of nature is the ground on which Shiva performs his cosmic dance. A Master knows everything without reacting to anything, which in an ordinary man would be an attitude of stupidity. If a Master uses the agitation which is around him to create and destroy

---

[3] "Doing" is used in the sense of genuine action freely undertaken and fully conscious. This is very far from what is customarily called "doing."

what must be destroyed, it becomes an energy guided by his wisdom since he draws it from a law known to him alone. This knowledge of a higher law is white, very lightly tinted. If a Master is conscious of this in his realization, he will make few mistakes. With whiteness he has full control over the whole spectrum of colors. That is why Yama, the Lord of Death, is always represented symbolically in white, which is higher knowledge. The buffalo on which he rides is pictured as black, which is the vital force, and his *Shakti* wears red which is the operative force.

Gurdjieff had this lightly tinted whiteness. He never stopped playing with all the colors of life; that is why fools cry out against him. Ouspensky, who was a philosopher, tried to stay in the whiteness he had discovered; but if you are the disciple responsible for the kitchen, your duty is to prepare the food. If you refuse to do this, you will be sent away by the Master or you will leave of your own accord and your refusal will be a weight that will burden you for years and possibly even crush you. Who can understand what a Master is teaching in five directions at once? And how could it be otherwise? In the tradition, Shiva has five faces with which to look at life.

Chaitanya said, "A man known for his worldly wisdom will find it difficult, despite all his intelligence, to understand the way of life and the actions of a man who has attained realization of the meaning of the cosmic laws." That is also why the *Katha Upanishad* and the *Bhagavad Gîtâ* speak of the Master who says to his beloved disciple, "No one can understand me, not even you. Be satisfied with praising me." Indeed, only the heart can recognize the Master. In this connection, I shall tell you some characteristic stories illustrating the extreme freedom of those free beings who play with the laws. I shall not give any names because in popular language they are always called "Khepâ" or

"Mast,"[4] which means "one who is mad." Who they are, none knows for those who live near them have completely forgotten their family name and where they came from.

Once upon a time Khepâ Bâbâ was in Benares in the middle of a crowd who was looking at him and watching how he was behaving, without daring to approach for if anyone bothered him, he would brandish his stick and hurl insults. One daring woman came towards him moaning, "Oh Maharaj, have pity on me." "Daughter of a whore!" Khepâ Bâbâ shouted at her. "Come here and I will rape you in the street in front of everyone!" She fled!

Khepâ Bâbâ had a jug of wine in front of him. He calmly drank it down to the last drop without saying a word. The people were stupefied at this impious act,[5] not understanding what was going on, but his disciples noticed that he had become white like Shiva; his body irradiated light. Khepâ Bâbâ was in ecstasy.

With his immense power and his heart of pure gold, Khepâ Bâbâ threw up almost insurmountable obstacles around him and created dangerous reefs provoking deep eddies in those living near him. Who was he? What do people expect from a Master? That he cleanse us of our prejudices; that he puncture the abscess of the ego; that he burn the featherbed of our laziness. All this Khepâ Bâbâ did in his uncouth way, for he himself was beyond good and evil. He constantly provoked people into facing themselves, into dwelling with themselves.

One day he ordered one of his favorite disciples to accompany him to Brindavan, which is one of the most sacred places of India, its atmosphere filled with the sweetness and

[4] In Hindi, the title "Mast" is given to the Sufis "gone mad," who constitute a separate group like the Bâuls.

[5] In India it is traditional for those who give themselves up to a spiritual search not to drink alcohol.

charm of the Child-Krishna. Kepâ Bâbâ sat down among the beggars on the side of the dusty road, a piece of cloth spread out in front of him. Passers-by threw alms into it, small coins or a handful of rice. According to what he received, Khepâ Bâbâ murmured a word or two of blessing or emitted an obscene swearword. Back at his hut, he tied up the coins in a rag and hung it on the wall. He lay down, but kept an eye on his meager treasure all night long like a miser, stick in hand. His disciples, silent and reproachful, watched him. At last Khepâ Bâbâ swore at them, "Are you criticizing me? Well then! Away with all of you! What keeps you here?"

"I couldn't leave," related his favorite disciple. "I remained standing there until daybreak, not understanding what was going on before me or in me; and when the Master got up, I followed him. I sat down behind him while he begged on the side of the road. Then the Master turned round and said to me in a serious voice, 'Take a good look, Tara, this is one aspect of the world, and I shall show you many others!'"

"On another occasion," continued the disciple, "Khepâ Bâbâ sent me to the village market to steal a goat. He had seen it while passing and wanted that one and no other. It was an easy thing to do. But I resisted. He insisted. I still refused. Then he shrugged his shoulders and went to sleep. I was so full of anguish that I felt drunk. I started to vomit. Finally, covered with shame, I went out, weeping and gritting my teeth, and stole the goat. It was not until later that I found out that all the goats supposedly belonging to this merchant were really Khepâ Bâbâ's own." One day Khepâ Bâbâ brutally chased away this beloved disciple. "Go away!" he shouted at him. "Fly now with your own wings!"

Among the disciples of Khepâ Bâbâ there was at Brindavan an illiterate villager, meek by nature and full of faith. With other *Vaishnavite* pilgrims, he subjected himself once a year to a severe discipline which consisted of going around the whole town bare foot, making prostrations after every few steps. At night the pilgrims rested but resumed their painful journey every morning at daybreak for fourteen days. The sun was blinding, the ground burned the soles of the feet, thirst and hunger were a constant torture. One night Khepâ Bâbâ happened to be at one of the stopping places where the pilgrims were sleeping. He called his disciple and asked him to prepare for him and others with him some wheat cakes (*chapatis*), insisting that they be very thin. The disciple went to light a brazier and began to knead the flour with water and salt. He made a pile of *chapatis* and brought them to his Guru. "What a fool you are!" said the Guru, and raising his stick, struck him full in the face. The disciple did not stir; his eyes never left the eyes of his Master. Then Khepâ Bâbâ caught him by the shoulder and pressed him to his bosom. He made him sit down by his side and made him eat first. This disciple became a great saint who died before Khepâ Bâbâ.

Khepâ Bâbâ wore his matted hair rolled into a bun on the top of his head. One of his disciples, imagining that he had jewels hidden in his hair, decided to poison him so as to get hold of them. One night he went stealthily to the corner of the house where the food was being prepared and put arsenic in the Guru's food. But he was caught in the act. Yelling, the others seized him and were about to beat him and throw him out.

"Don't chase that man out!" cried Khepâ Bâbâ.

"Then you must do it yourself," shouted the disciples angrily.

"What has he done?"

"He tried to poison you with arsenic!"

"Ah!" exclaimed Khepâ Bâbâ, "and you poison me daily

with your quarrels . . . Get away, all of you! Out of here!"
The uproar stopped. The man remained.

It is difficult, indeed, to understand the actions of a man
who has come to realization in himself of the cosmic laws;
his life is lived under everyone's eyes day and night; his life
is absolutely untainted with egoism. Khepâ Bâbâ, with all
the knots of his heart untied, let things happen naturally.
What did it matter that someone wanted to kill him and others
to avenge him? The laws have always worked in the same
way, in *prakriti*, which is always the same. In my *âshram*
in Assam the contrasts were just as violent. What is a Guru
for, if not to tear us apart from ourselves? My co-disciples
were often hungry while the Master had all he could possibly
want. Those who could not bear it left. To others it all
seemed natural; we were intoxicated by his presence. We
lived on his knowledge.

XIII.

Life—Death

The Bâul always sees life on a background of death. What is meant here by "death" is complete freedom from all bondage and limitations. Life by its nature possesses and binds, but death makes us free. If we could guard in ourselves the quietness of death, we would have access to creative intelligence. This is the level of objectivity on the moral plane.

I am not speaking of physical death, the inevitable last scene of life's drama, but of death in Shiva, that is, of the transcendence that supports the creative rhythm of life. We can "build up" all sorts of things in ordinary life, but to create we must be liberated by voluntary death in Shiva. Creative vision belongs only to him who, seeing beyond the dance of life, dares to look within himself into the Void. Then what does he see? The beginning and the end, the seed from which life springs, and the flowers under which life's adventure ends. He sees the arc of the Void which broods over both.

How desirable it would be to feel in oneself the great strength that lies dormant behind the word *Mâyâvâda!*[1] *Mâyâ* is neither illusion nor relativity. Alas! People do not wish to understand it, for these words explain the passivity, the sleep, and the recurrent nature of *prakriti*, whereas *Mâyâ* is free will, the freedom to create. *Mâyâ* is the idea of life giving rise to multiple forms, just as the word "flower" gives rise to endless forms in the mind.

To which form should one be attached? To none and yet to all. Imagine that you are impartial, not attached to one form or another, not dogmatic about one form or another. Then every form will delight you, for in each you will see the incarnation of a life-idea. And *Mâyâ* is this exuberance of creation.

India exists in various forms, some beautiful, some ugly, yet this dualistic distinction becomes unreal as soon as movement upward toward the light is recognized. Our life-impulse is witness to the reality of this.

The Buddha said that reality is the Void itself and that ultimate existence issues from non-existence. All we can try is to bring the idea of death to the very heart of life, for to know that everything will finally sink into the Void is a great relief. We work with a smile and a feeling of freedom only if we know that nothing will last forever. Then we are like children building castles of sand on the shore of time.

All *râja-yoga* is a study of death, how consciously to accept the living inertia and dare to face it. He who dies valiantly in war, or in self-sacrifice, touches a plane of consciousness which, at best, corresponds to the vital being. He who sees death approach with bitterness knows what the opposite of sweetness is. He who sees death approach with sweetness

[1] A theory according to which multiplicity or manifestation is unreal.

knows the opposite of bitterness. This is a much higher plane of consciousness.

The discipline to follow in life is to harmonize the levels of the inner being facing existence, without identification, without thought, by means of breathing exercises (*prâ-nâyama*)[2] when they have become familiar and natural. Then the Void is the return to the beginning, the matrix of Life.

At the moment of death, all that is matter returns to matter, all that is energy returns to primordial energy. Only those very rare beings escape this dispersion who work consciously to bring their different "I's" together around the central axis and who free themselves from the grip of *prakriti*. For them, real Existence (*Sat*) continues.

He who is conscious of this process progresses slowly and without any "will" whatsoever, for unification around the axis is not the result of efforts but is made possible by a new "substance" which arises when the right time comes. This substance is known exactly, and is described in different ways in the *Upanishads*.

At the moment of physical death or of passage to a lighter density, *Purusha* is perceptible in the vibration of *Shakti*. It is a moment of transubstantiation, a function of the spirit informed by sensation.

When you are face to face with death, do not struggle. Let yourself glide. The impulse that will carry you away is cosmic. It is not comparable to any life-force. It is written that "Death is the last of the sacrifices." To reach this point, the sacrifice of life has to have been made long before. Then, in the last sacrifice, there is not even the waiting for death. It is simply the "life-death state."

As you progress through life, you will progress through death. Do not struggle. It is with this attitude of openness that one can hear "the call of the secret companion," that is,

---

[2] *Prânâyama* are the breathing exercises that lead to a knowledge of the inner order.

the voice of death. What follows no longer has any meaning; one enters into a new field of forces. Does one know what one is going to do when one arrives on earth? Why would the same thing not apply after death? There may be as many solutions in death as there are in life. One follows, it is certain, a road opened by an exact law.

The monk's renunciation (*sannyâsa*) truly signifies death. It is one of the great traditional ways.

A theory of death and *sannyâsa* existed among the Vedic sages even before the advent of Buddhism. Thus Buddhism, with its great monastic tradition, is a kind of organized *sannyâsa*. The monks were recluses nourished from Buddhism by way of the *Sâmkhya* philosophy, with its idealization of Shiva. In short, Shiva and Buddha are the same ideal expressed by the sound: "*A-Ham*"—which includes the whole being and the whole ego, this sound being composed of two letters —the first and the last of the Sanskrit alphabet.[3]

It is written in the *Purânas* that the first letter of the alphabet is Vishnu, or life, and that the last is Shiva, or death. Therefore the two states, life-death, are united by the great *mantra* "Hari-Hara," whose meaning is "to live a full life." But no one understands it. How many honest monks are there on that terrible road of destruction (*pralaya*)? Very few. Most of them wear the ocher robe of renunciation as an emblem of what they are attempting to reach without being any the less attached to what they still possess. Sometimes it is the "idea" itself represented by their robe. The real *sannyâsin* is the one described in the *Bhagavad Gîtâ*, who goes about with no outer sign by which he can be recognized and who often wears different masks in the world.

The question "What exists after death?" was formulated by the *Rishis* of the *Upanishads*.

[3] *Aitareya Âranyaka*, II 3.8.

Ramprasad, in the eighteenth century, gave an answer to this question in one of his songs, which even today is on everybody's lips:

> . . . Do you know, my brother,
> what man becomes after death?
> There remains but a water bubble . . .
> Spurting from the wave, it sinks again into the foam
> forming but one with the immense ocean.

If we accept this philosophy of the water bubble leaving the matrix of Great Nature and returning to her bosom, there is naturally neither paradise, nor hell, nor soul. The question "What becomes of the soul after death?" was asked long ago in the *Katha Upanishad*[4] and the answer given is exactly the same.

If this answer is *felt* to the point where the entire being is filled, all other values become true in its light.

[4] II, Sec. 1.15.

XIV

Letters

January 18, 1951

Don't look up to man for help. Behind every man, see the power in whose hands the man is only an instrument. No man can help or harm the divine will that you are. A smile and silence. Yes, that will be your response to everything that comes to you. Things are good or bad only to the diseased or prejudiced mind which automatically criticizes everything. They are ripples of power to one who sees and creates.

Feel that *Shakti* within you—the *Shakti* called *"Mahisha-mardini,"*[1] who smilingly crumples in her hands the enraged and obstinate buffalo, the demon of ignorance. Smile, but at the same time crush and transform!

[1] Name of the goddess Durga, one of the aspects of the active energy of Shiva.

March 25, 1951

Remain calm and mistress of yourself. Draw yourself in. Create from within your being. Live in the Void. Do not let life's shocks disturb you nor the questions arising from them.

Make every shock a source of intense spiritual strength that will create within you a form hard as granite, white as the snows of Haïmavatî, the consolidation of power on earth—the dream of my whole life.

April 2, 1951

If you are feeling lonely, it is because you do not yet know who you are. You must not depend upon people or things around you. The day you really come to know your own self, you will become impersonal.

The utmost that can be predicted about you then is that you are a force or an idea.

Yes, your background is activity. Why should you not be yourself? Don't imitate others. Everyone must be guided by his own destiny (*dharma*). You know the secret. Let the Void be your support; lean back on the cushion in the Void.

Let the episode that troubled you be buried quickly. Whatever gets heavy and troublesome, it is best to send it down again to the bosom of Mother Earth. But this must be done quite consciously. Laying down a burden does not mean to reject it. The earth will know how to turn the deposit into good manure. Even rotten things can be turned to the best use in that way.

March 22, 1952

As time goes on, how everything appears so distant and fantastic! I remember how I used to feel like this when I was young and labored night and day for my Guru. But for whom am I laboring now? For my dream.

I don't know if I shall see it fulfilled while I am on earth. Only I feel that I am diving deeper and deeper into her bowels like a meandering root. I am thirstily sucking her sap and sending it up to flower and bloom, which perhaps I shall never see. I can only say, "A great austerity (*tapasya*) has come upon me."

April 20, 1952

This is how I understand your return to "life." It is in tune with the rhythm of your personal destiny (*svadharma*); you must be true to it. My loyalty to "Death" (*Yama*) will be the background against which your "life" will shine.

As for me, I have my "work" that I have to do, and there is the "dream" that I shall always be dreaming, without ever hoping to see it realized. I have felt the pulse of India and do not expect any big result. These are the days of preparing nothing more than manure. We sow only to mow down the young plants. The great seed will be cast when the soil is ready. I see the mighty tree in my dream that will exist one day. It is my God—but only a Dream-God.

I am carried in my work neither by hope nor by despondence. It is like the mighty stream of Brahmaputra moving slowly and majestically with hardly any ripple on it. I like this rhythm in which sound the words, "I am alone with the Alone." It is not joy. It is peace and a sweet, sad love beaded with sparkling tears.

April 27, 1952

. . . If a time of dissolution (*pralaya*) were to come, what would be your reaction to the "ugly" face of truth? Remember that truth is always beautiful because it gives freedom, and we must be free within to have a real taste of life.

I was looking today at a picture of Shrî Râmana Maharshi. For sixty years he did nothing. He simply lived and stared

into the Void. This is good! I have also been reading Shrî
Aurobindo's *Savitrî*, a staggering pyramid of fantasies! For
forty years he had been a recluse, spinning dreams around
him. That is also good! I like them both. They lived in their
own way—one in the nudity of Death, the other in writing
The Life Divine—are they not the faces of the same Inex-
pressible? Well, we have to live, to grow, to bloom, to seed,
and then to die. Let us do it with grace, like the season's
flowers!

December 3, 1952

You must have received news of me by this time en route.
As yet there has been no flux of visitors. The weather is not
too cold.

The calm of Haïmavatî remains intact. Have I lost my grip
on life? Perhaps not. The phrase "spiritual existentialism" we
coined has become so real here. I can exactly imagine how
you will feel when you come into the crowd. It will be there
and yet it will not be. The soul like a little child, simply
looking at things with wondering eyes—not evaluating, not
passing judgment on anything, not bound by a sense of duty
and yet silently active in radiating her simple joy of living;
how wonderful!

Love wears a new face then; suddenly it becomes secure
in the depths. I love because I exist. I possess everything
because I am nothing. My love is a light that gently kisses
the drooping brow of sorrow and passes on. It embraces
everything but sticks to nothing.

You remember the story I told you of Devahutî, the mother
of Kapila, who had known life in a womanly fullness and
then known the Void in its manly grandeur and at the end
of her earthly existence had chosen to change herself into a
sparkling stream. That is the eternal Woman. I can't picture
her as Mother today. She is the child who holds the gods
on her tiny palm.

April 5, 1953

Yes, life in Haïmavatî has been full. It has been like a pure flame burning all dross and shooting upward, melting in the Void. The material Haïmavatî has died in order to be changed into a luminous idea that will never die. I shall never forget the sacrifice you made to Her, not to any institution but to the idea—an idea beyond the comprehension of the mind, but how real! The last year has been wonderful, though outwardly it was a movement of dissolution. But inwardly, what wonderful freedom and ease and power. Have you not felt that?

And now let me tell you that Almora is really a land of dissolution (*pralaya*). This year there has not been one drop of rain for over two months. The water shortage is terrible and we have to wait another two months until the rains come. Everything is scorched, dried up, brittle. The skin cracks as it does in winter. But how wonderful it is! I feel neither dead nor alive, but in strange communion with existence. The only thing that counts is true action. All opposites have faded away in a luminous haze which envelops everything and swallows it up. I do not know what will remain.

May 1, 1953

Always rest within the Void and you will understand. It is understanding that counts. Really it is something like working with intelligence. Very few people do that. Actions do not matter at all. Your action benefits none but your own self. If your actions clear your vision, they are all right. If not—well, it is all illusion (*Mayâ*). Only the Void will tell you.

June 14, 1953

I am in absolute peace these days. Work is also vanishing though I work the whole day. There is no sense in working for something; you *be* the work itself. Not to *become*, it is simply *being*. A tree does not know what it is going to be-

come, but every moment it simply *is*. Do you call that unconsciousness, stupidity? What is our consciousness but a
feverish dream? When we awake—and we really awake (not
simply pass from one dream to another dream, which we
fondly cherish as awakening)—we no longer become, but we
are. The whole secret of life is to pin your faith on that being,
knowing that it is insensible, it is the Void.

The other day, while I was carelessly turning over the pages
of my volume of *Rigveda*, I suddenly came upon a passage of
Saunaka, a very old index-maker of the *Vedas*. He said, "There
is only one God and that God is the Sun." It gave me a
violent start. It was as if Saunaka was nodding his head and
saying: "We all felt like that, and that produced the *Vedas*."
And the sun said, "I have been shining for millions and millions
of years and I shall go on shining for millions of years. As
long as I shine and don't become too hot for people to live
on the earth, well, you can go on weaving dreams of *âshrams*
and Gurus, of divinization, and so on!"

Can you feel, at the bottom of your woman's heart, that you
are nothing but a bit of solar energy, dead and stiffened, and
yet trying to warm up into the radiance of that solar orb? And
if you succeed, you will be Savitrî, which literally means
nothing but the solar energy.

And the sun, is he going to live for all eternity? Of course
not. Every evening he goes down and I pull a chair into the
yard and stare at the fading crest of Shyama Devî,[2] which
looks so strangely like the heaving breast of a woman lying
on her back. I see the dead earth in her. The darkness swallows everything. And then nothing remains but the Void.

Can you unite that death with life? Only then you will live!
I have told you of nothing but death. You must know him
(*Yama*) and be married to him before you go back to life—
to your life. Follow the curve of life, don't struggle against
it. Only know that you are secure in the Void that is beyond.

[2] The peak of the hill above Almora, below which stands Haïmavatî.

And then have a good smile at life. I have always been a cipher to you because I knew that this is the only truth.

August 3, 1953

I am so happy to know that you are leaving India feeling empty and stripped of everything. That is the way to create life! You will be bringing back something other than fine, reassuring words—a pulsating life that cannot be seen or heard, but can only be felt as a vibration. Give yourself up completely. Return to the earth again, and from your self-effacement you will be giving life to thousands of sprouting seeds. Be the very spirit of the earth—the patient mother who suckles her children without uttering a word.

The unknown is before you, but the known is in you. And that which knows will master that which does not know. If you know yourself, you also know your universe, which will be molded by your understanding. May Haïmavatî be with you always, for it will be your strength, your *Shakti*.

September 17, 1953

May your return to the West be a new birth, in every sense of the term. You have learned from life, you have learned even more from death. Now let death be your Master and Lord. It is safe to walk with him along the path of life. To possess nothing, not even your thoughts, to know that everything is and simply to look at them—asking nothing, refusing nothing—that is the secret of the "no-mind." Let not life but death plant within you whatever he likes. You have simply to accept and make it fruitful with the sap of your being.

All creations are in the Void. So, there can be absolutely no frustration in any worker who has known the Void. To know this is not to quarrel, not to worry, not to hurry in getting things done. Things arrange themselves automatically around him, not according to any human plan, mind you! And the Divine has no plan at all. He is like a child playing with creation and destruction at random because he is above both. The *Vedas* say, "He is death and immortality is his shadow. All is *Mâyâ*." There is complete security and freedom in the knowledge of that. But this is a truth that should not be spoken about, it must be felt.

As for me, you know I can best be of use to you if I am impersonal. You can think of me in whatever way you like, only if that leads you to your complete freedom. If it leads to the Void, then relations are true; if not—beware! If you have made all I have given you your own so that no trace of me is left in them, then you have understood. And I can be silent again, knowing I have done my part.

September 20, 1953

So! Gurdjieff has been keeping you company during your voyage?

We have lost the esoteric and the occult sense by being civilized and it has not been for our good. The upward evolution is not without difficulty. We have to reclaim what we have lost. The other day I was thinking that if evolution is true and we have passed through a vegetable stage of life, then why did we lose that power of changing inorganic matter into food? Why can we not suck our life from Mother Earth as the plants do? If we know how the plants do that, why can we not get back the technique in our own bodies? Much of occultism is thus going back to the bosom of the earth, to hunt for the lost continent of Atlantis. Yes, we have to deal with "mass" and "matter," but we have to do it in a spiritual way. A long and tiresome process, of course. But still we have to do it.

September 29, 1953

When you become one with a thing, that thing no longer exists for you and yet something may happen in you—a manifestation that is, of course, an illusion (*Mâyâ*)—an in-scrutable mystery. It is good to know that life is a mystery. I do not laugh at it like Gurdjieff nor do I glorify it like Shrî Aurobindo. I simply smile.

Of course death is the greatest experience that we can have while in life. Cannot one part of you live and the other part die? Life will then be only like the twinkling of a star sur-rounded by a great abyss of death and darkness.

It is good to feel this darkness within you—the unmani-fested which you can call Kâlî-the-Mother or any other name you like. Life means nothing if you know that there is death behind you, ready to absorb you again, as the great Void is absorbing every moment millions of seers, of "those who know." To know this while living, "to carry death into every movement of your life," is the consummation of life's pur-pose. Death is peace, death is silence, death is power. Don't laugh, don't glorify, only smile. Smile because you know.

From Shillong, April 26, 1954

A week ago I shifted to the new Haïmavatî at Shillong. I am gradually settling down. It is a small cottage, quite simple, where one can live as in a mountain cave. It is com-manding a fine view of vast pine forests. The house is built on a piece of land belonging to the Khasias.[3] As a result, here I am living right in the heart of the dissidence which is stirring this country and I am a subject not of the Assam government but of the Khasia Parvati. So I have automatically become a rebel, which I always was by nature!

The house consists of three tiny rooms the size of the one we used as a refectory in Almora. There will be a water tap and electric light. What luxury! The place is extremely quiet. My neighbors are very poor, peaceful Khasias. Their small boy will come every day to clean the dishes with ashes.

[3] An independent tribe of Assam.

My work routine will be the same as in Almora. As you see, for a definite period, I have returned to the "cave life" I like.

May 9, 1954

In my last letter I gave you news about the new Haïmavatî that has grown up here. As I am writing, I am looking at the landscape through the window, a strange mixture of the soft scene of Lohaghat and the rugged beauty of Almora. I am alone, completely alone. There is a small boy now who draws water for me every day. I cook for myself and do my washing.

There are a few pupils nearby. You know them. U. sees to it that nothing interferes with my work. A. has been a wonderful help. He is copying all the manuscripts before they go off to the printer. They come twice a week to read *Sâmkhya* with me. M. comes every Wednesday to take lessons in Sanskrit. So you see it is just like what we had planned in Almora, with the difference that now I am doing all these things without the slightest idea of building up anything. I know that these students may fail me any moment. But I have to give what I have, and I give it not to the person, but to the spirit behind. Thus I serve Haïmavatî.

Haïmavatî is a living idea, whether we are referring to the place where you live in Europe or to the house in Almora. The same is true of the house in Shillong. So there the house in the Swiss Himalayas and the house in the Eastern Himalayas. Everywhere the living idea is that of the "secret cave," the temple in the heart of man in which *Purusha* is absorbed in himself.

I am happy to know that your work is recognized and supported. Accept any help that gives you freedom on the explicit condition that you free yourself of every hindrance that might prevent you from serving fully. If you do it consciously and silently, *Purusha* will uphold you. Never betray and you will be in harmony with yourself—even if things become difficult.

November 28, 1954

Continue to live the life of Haïmavatî and you will discover that there has been absolutely no break in the flow of *Shakti*. During these last two years,[4] there was only an eddy and *Shakti* now flows on as evenly as before.

Bring to your friends the spirit of Haïmavatî, which is the secret India you have known, but do not stress that it is India. A mother nurses her child not with the food she herself eats, but with her milk, with her own life sap into which she has transformed the material food. You have passed barriers, found your freedom. Be human, which means incarnating the Divine. May the discipline of *Sâmkhya* and the spirit of the Bâul sustain your strength, your *Shakti*.

December 19, 1954

Man is growing. There will come a day when we shall know true spiritual democracy, everyone standing on his own feet and hailing one another "Brother!" No Masters, no Gurus. Science, logic, democracy are all tending toward the spiritual-democratic movement. When man has learned to be spiritually free from all dogmas, learned not to lean on any staff but on his own feet, then the Vedic spirit will dawn upon him making the heaven and earth one.

There is one trait in the European mind which we here have lost for the last two thousand years—it is the love of nature as the pagan loves it, that is, for its own sake. In this trait lies one of the greatest secrets of releasing the bonds of the soul. This romanticism in a European soul is something very real which, unfortunately, is considered as something going against spirituality. The cause lies in the Semitic idea

---

[4] Since my return to Europe.

that this world is a created thing and not God himself, this latter idea being the old Vedic idea which we ourselves lost after the eleventh century, and which Rabindranath Tagore brought back to us, without himself knowing he was renewing something which was a part of our own heritage.

Always make people feel that God, soul, and Nature are one, that spiritual growth is not an intellectual process but a life process—an all-round growth. It is not the attainment of something distant but a flowering of what is within. Remove all obstacles, conventions, superstitions, and you will find that you are flooded with light which was just waiting for the windows of your heart to be opened.

Love the youthful spirit in man. Therein lies another secret. Adolescence is the flowering period of life, represented by Krishna. Our whole aim should be to make adolescence more and more conscious. You can help the beauty of a well-adjusted family life. That is true spirituality because it is worship of a life divine.

August 13, 1955

Put out strong roots into your native soil. Go ahead with the work that connects you with your search. Make it a play of *Shakti*. Where there is complete detachment, there is a spontaneous flow of energy. Your way of working with a group impersonally is fine. You have caught the spirit. Feeling deeply within oneself the "real I," to live it and radiate it spontaneously—that is the law of divine work.

As far as possible, give up all outer forms in your relations with people. Of course, it is impossible not to use forms—gestures, movements, and words. But these are only preliminaries. What you are really doing is absorbing and then radiating. Always look beyond the forms and you will find *prakriti*—a vast ocean of energy coming in waves that take on various aspects. Absorb *prakriti* and remain calm. The only thing that counts is to *be*—and then let radiation take place.

February 18, 1956

I can't send you a photograph because no one has taken a picture of me lately. You can picture me as you saw me last. Perhaps I have become thinner. But the light burns bright. Only I feel more drawn inwards. A great solitude is swallowing me and I like it. People are crowding around me here from morning to evening, always asking questions, the same questions. Sometimes I go to the cinema, which is taboo for a *sâdhu*. Am I blasphemous?

March 11, 1956

If you feel that India is calling you, of course you will come back. But you must not create circumstances. Be drawn by the stream of events. If you have courage enough to live your own inner life and at the same time let yourself be carried by the stream of life without your own will, then the whole world is yours.

You can live without any attachment anywhere you are wanted. It might be there just as well as here. You just live the life of the Bâül. He arrives somewhere, works with all his heart, and packs off as soon as he is not wanted. His inner life is all he possesses. If he joins a group, he works for it just as if he were joining in the play of children at recreation and he quietly drops away when the children are tired or simply don't want to play any more.

If you dare to conceive the movement of life like this, you are on the right side. But if you think you have something to do, that you are necessary, then you will once more be caught by the snare of *Mâyâ*. Are you able to be free like the Bâüls? Not intellectually, but in activity. If so, perhaps some day you will find a "cause" to serve, just as I have found mine after I had played with things for years. And even then, you must remain free. You must not forget that this "cause" is still a play of *Mâyâ*, who can devour you. The Void alone is ultimate reality.

August 24, 1956

Do not be attached to anything! Do not clutch onto anything! Only like this will life's current lead you without shock to the vast ocean of the Void. Real self-observation is exactly to find again and again the sensation of the Void in the very heart of life's struggle. This is the sensation that can illuminate death when it comes to us. Spiritual discipline implies a merciless struggle in the reality of life. Then one is conscious of what real Existence is, of which life and death are the two poles.

March 15, 1959

Simply float on. Do things as if you had nothing to do. When I am in a fix, I simply become blank and wait. Great Nature does the same.

It is best to forget everything from time to time, even for a whole day. Then things rush back in by themselves, as if they were brought by life's current. One has to learn the trick of being able to float. A stream never flows backwards.

It is good to know that you are slowly and steadily striking your roots into the soil of your country. The day will come when the principles of *Sâmkhya* will deliver the European mind from its present dreams and psychoreligious nightmares.

Last week, a young man who comes to see me every Sunday said that your book *My Life With a Brahmin Family* was on sale in one of the local bookshops in Gauhatî. He stood at the counter turning page after page, thrilled by this picture of the life that is his, and almost finished the whole book.

"It was so engrossing!" was his remark. But he had no money to buy it.

May 26, 1964 (after a serious illness)

I am still extremely weak. This enforced holiday was a blessing in disguise. The experience of suffering has been wonderful. It has opened up new vistas of truth and welded all past experiences into a solid whole. So it comes to this, "All is Brahman,"[5] be it pain or joy, life or death, light or darkness." Beyond everything is the silent Void, the only objective reality, which engulfs all subjective appearances. Wonderful!

June 13, 1964

The monsoons have started. The garden is in full bloom with summer flowers. What a beauty! And in four months I am going to leave it all behind me, with a laugh. I have been quietly happy here and shall be so wherever I go. The name Haïmavatî remains. I leave the house in the care of a friend who nursed me so patiently during my long illness.

I feel a new life pouring into me. Not that I am looking forward to any conspicuous result—no, not that. It is simply the fullness of the Void, the pure gaze that looks through the *Mâyâ* of it all, the ineffable smile of the Buddha serenity. *Prakriti* is wonderful! She is so prolific in her inventions and she keeps *Purusha* always spellbound with the novelties she ushers in from day to day. Oh, it is a joy to BE, simply to BE.

Do not get stuck! Flow on, not even caring if you reach the Ocean or not.

April 25, 1965

It is a good sign you are dissatisfied with yourself. Self-complacence would have meant death. Dissatisfaction is the

[5] *Sarvam Khalvidam Brahmâ.*

stirring of the great *Shakti*, which is making you feel that you have not done enough.

Take this dissatisfaction itself as a part of the great game you are playing. Don't be troubled by it. Take it easily, as you have taken so many things. And live quietly and deeply. Live as if you are not living, work as if you are not working, talk as if you are not talking, think as if you are not thinking. Then the great *Shakti* lying deep within you and causing these stirrings of the heart will reveal herself. You will be taken up by her and be one with her. Then you will know what you have to know. Non-existence will then become the fountainhead of bubbling existence. Never to be satisfied is one of the main features of *Sâmkhya* discipline.

June 21, 1965

I am still in the dark about the friend who is building the new Haïmavatî in the former bed of the Ganges near Calcutta. He has given me lifelong freedom to use the house. According to the Scriptures, a serpent never burrows a hole; it lives in a hole made by others and leaves it when it likes. That is also what the Bâül says from the heart of his freedom.

If you come to see me, you will again have a taste of life as it was in Lohaghat. We will follow the same pattern of life again, but it will not be so quiet, as we have neighbors—all peasants, Hindus and Muslims living together like brothers, so much so that you cannot distinguish them. From the South comes the call to prayer by muezzins, from the North conches, bells and the chants of *kirtans*. And no breaking heads over the modes of praying to the same God.

PART III

THE BÂÜLS OF BENGAL

Shrî Anirvân

The Bâuls play an indispensable role in Bengal. It would be easy to point a finger at them saying, "Madmen drunk with God," or even, "Illiterate beggars in the vain pursuit of a dream"; nevertheless, it is from them that Rabindranath Tagore derived much of his inspiration. In fact, the great poet collected the words of many of their songs and many of their touchingly simple melodies.[1] While they remain outside the orthodox traditions of India, the Bâuls nevertheless represent one of the underground currents of spiritual life which remain intensely alive. This current can be traced to a time even before that of the Vedic religions.

The name "Bâul," however, first appears in the literature

[1] Rabindranath Tagore spoke publicly of the Bâuls for the first time in a public lecture at the University of Calcutta and in his Hilbert Lectures published in *The Religion of Man*.

of Bengal only in the fifteenth century. It seems to derive
from the word "bâtula" (*vâtula* in Sanskrit), meaning "he
who is beaten by the winds"; he, that is, who abandons
himself to all his impulses. From that point to madness is
only a step! But this ecstatic madness has its origin in God,
and its aim also in God!

The Bâüls must not be thought of as forming a particular
sect. *Sâdhakas* who follow a spiritual discipline and belong to
all sorts of brotherhoods and religious groups may become
Bâüls if they are so disposed. Chinese philosophy, in its close-
ness to nature, has perhaps the nearest approach to Bâüls
in its Ch'an, Zen adepts, who so delight in paradox. The
dominant note that marks the Bâüls is their complete spiritual
freedom, which is an organic force without the slightest
pretension. In ordinary life, thanks to their utter non-con-
ventionality, they are typical freethinkers, who have unwit-
tingly become a free institution. There is no outer connection
between them of any kind.

They are recognizable because they generally wear long
robes—though these are not distinctive of any existing religious order. They let their hair and beards grow. Since for
them the Divine is formless and mythology a dead letter, they
are never seen making obeisance to any image or to any
human being, no matter how perfect he may be! They no
longer belong to any caste.

The Bâül's philosophy is not formulated in any sacred writings. He does not depend on any tradition. Above all else
he lets himself be guided by intuition.

The Bâüls' only means of expression is extemporaneous
singing which voices their intimate spiritual experience. There
are as many Hindu Bâüls as there are Muslim. Escaping from
all orthodox forms, their lives are completely integrated in
the unity that exists between teacher (Guru) and pupil
(*shishya*). In fact, Muslim Gurus are known to initiate

Hindus, and Hindu Gurus to initiate Muslims. This inner relationship is ordained by God.

There are monks, ascetics, and married men among the Bâuls. They go from village to village, singing, with their *ektaras*—a simple one-stringed instrument—and their small drums called *dubkis*. At certain times of the year and in certain propitious places, the Bâuls come together periodically in a big fair (*mela*) where the songs and dances continue day and night for as long as the gathering lasts. On these occasions there are no rites of worship and no oral teaching, for these mystic poets attach no importance to anything except the vibration of souls—nothing else.

The spiritual discipline of the Bâuls is centered on the cult of the man in whom God is called *Maner manûsh*—"He who lives in the heart." This god has only one attribute. He is all love! There is no mention here of God the Creator nor of God the Destroyer.

One of the ways of reaching God is to give oneself up to a Guru who becomes the link between man and the Divine. So the Guru is highly venerated and respected, but teacher and pupil remain perfectly free on both sides with no conditions between them of loyalty or obedience, with no fixed obligation or responsibility.

The spiritual discipline of the Bâul is solely the flowering of the inner being, of the constant presence of God. There is no search for any support from outer things. Just on that account, their discipline, which begins with the body, requires that the body, which plays the role of instrument, be kept extremely pure, for the body is "the temple of God." "*In this body lives the Man; if you call him, He will answer you.*" It is actually a technique for seeking God in oneself by using the instrument of the body that God gave us: "*God made Himself man; in the perfect man who is the Guru, man is made divine, so the ideal of God can be attained in our own bodies.*" The cult of the Bâul, in short, is spiritualized humanism.

The spiritual attitude of the Bâul has found in Bengal a terrain well prepared to favor the growth of his philosophy's three principal ideas.

The idea of God as love has been enriched by all the adepts of *bhakti-yoga* and by the *Vaishnavites* for whom Krishna is "He who lives in the heart." The idea of the Guru as the perfect man who, while still a man, has attained the highest goals, is a direct contribution of Islam. In Hinduism, in fact, the Guru is greater than all the gods, is himself divine. For the Bâul, the veneration due to the Guru (*guruvada*) is deeply rooted in the ancient history of Bengal, where it was well known long before the advent of Buddhism—that is, in the cult of the *siddhas*. What survives today of this cult of the *siddhas*, of Buddhism and of Islam, has been transmuted into a harmonious composite in which the Bâuls come in contact with the Absolute through ecstatic love. The idea of the body as the temple of God comes directly from the *hatha* cult which is the basis of *hatha-yoga*. The Bâuls, in fact, are acquainted with a whole science of the body called *dehatattva* (which is no more than the science of *kundalinî* and of the *chakras* of the *hatha yogins*), which is practiced by Hindus and Muslims alike.

These characteristics of the Bâuls, which in our day form the link between Hindu and Muslim, are the pure product of the ancient non-conformist schools of Buddhism which laid enormous emphasis on metaphysical aspirations: "What is the first truth?" (*shunya*), and on pure experience: "What is it that is born in me?" (*sahaja*). These ideas are still alive for the Bâuls, who speak freely and willingly of *sahaja*. Pure experience is the great motive of their lives. Thus the non-orthodox mysticism of medieval India forms the background for the modern Bâuls, and the saints of Northern India, such as Kabir and Dadu, were certainly Bâüls. If we go back even further, we can connect the Bâüls directly with the mysterious *Vrâtya* cult of the *Artharva Veda*.

Most Bâüls are illiterate and come from the poorest ranks of society. But they also include learned Brahmins who have been rejected by their caste and Muslims excommunicated by their orthodoxy. Many Sufis have also become Bâüls through fear of persecution, saying: "We escape from orthodoxy (*shariyat*) in order to follow Truth (*Haqiqat*)."

These Bâüls are scattered over the entire country. Recently a Muslim Bâül even turned up in the mountains of Almora. He plucked the string of his *ektara* and repeated with every breath the holy Names of Râma, of Allah, of Krishna, of Buddha. When people showed some surprise, he began to sing:

> All these Names are the same Name,
> the only one which lives in the heart.
> O my brothers, why should we quarrel?
> He is everywhere, He nameless
> He, everywhere the same . . .

and, he added with some irony: "Now, I will tell you what is happening in the great world. . . ." And immediately he began to compose some sort of satirical verse scoffing at the political news of the day! "Why are you always singing?" he was asked. He replied:

> Because we were born singing birds in order to sing;
> we don't know how to walk on the ground
> but with wings spread, in the sky, we soar . . .

Mystic Songs

I

Take the lamp from the Master's hands
   and go down into the black abyss
   awaken your senses
   to the yoga of the "I" made free
   for you this will be
   the dawn of the supreme mystery.

Beatific visions
   will fill your heart
   beyond the measurable
   there where the worlds dance
   there where blooms the lotus of the thousand petals
     in whose halo
     you will know
   the mystic union of delights.

Between the existent
   and the non-existent
   the space is love . . .

Anonymous

II

The lotus of the heart
   blooms far from here
mysterious
   hidden by time's ages.
It is this that has made a slave of You
and of me also, my Adored One!

This lotus blossoms
   again and again
deathless flowering,
the honey flowing from it
an intoxicating sweetness,
the bee that eats it
   can no longer fly away . . .
It is this that has made a slave of You
   and of me also, my Adored One!

Neither You nor I have any wish
to tear ourselves away from this embrace!
Go away if You can, my Adored One!

Anonymous

III

Is my Beloved
a creaking axle
forever grinding and moaning?
Oh! speak to me of Your silence,
my Master, my Adored,
show me the path of silence
leading
to the Lotus of the Void . . .

The moon and the stars
forever ride the sky
—soundlessly
in Your silence . . .

Anonymous

IV

"Lord, show me, I beg,
how in the same man
guru and lover are but one?"

"If you live pure and sober,
experiencing divine delights,
some day, you will know it . . .
Lock after lock
defends the dwelling place of Darkness
in the inmost depths of being,
—and beyond.
But if the dazzling light of day
dawns in the waves of ecstasy
the luminous Darkness vanishes . . ."

At the threshold of the ninth dwelling
—O inconceivable mystery,
must I reveal to you
the Mother of mothers
the majestic, eternal Mother? . . .

Lalan Fakir

V

O my Beloved
who in Your heart
feel all the pain of mine,
why, tell me, does my unquiet soul
aspire to Your sweet peace?
My secret soul, evenly,
slowly, pursues its aim . . .

But my impatient heart
is troubled,
bursts into heavy sobbing . . .
The soul shudders,
the bitter tears flow.
"Come, my loved one, come . . ."
is the seductive call!

The tide attracts the waters,
the sea, the source of rivers.
So does the heart's poison
become pure nectar . . .

Anonymous

VI

To Krishna

You and I dance
O my King
in the mad gaiety of Holi[1]
—ecstasy of our souls.

Am I alone
bitten by desire?
No! my Adored,
You also languish with it!

To give Your joy
You need my smiles;
that Your song may be known
I must be its flute!

So that my whole body may be
the cradle of Your delight,
O my Adored.
Now it is for You
to kneel before me—
come beg my love . . .

Anonymous

[1] A spring festival during which colored waters are played with.

VII

At the turn of the river
a call rang out,
the call of an unknown Voice:
"Stop, boatman!
Make your boat fast,
rest a moment . . ."

"No! No! I cannot stop
the current carries me away . . ."

In this endless voyage
what must become of me? . . .
The eddies tug my boat away
and my desire is in the call . . .
O Master, I beg You,
take the helm!

Drive out the anguish
of Your suffering Jaga
Lord . . .

Jaga, the boatman

VIII

Beaten by the waves
laid low by the hard winds:
O Murshid
I take refuge in You!

In the west the storm growls
the clouds pile up in masses,
my battered boat trembles,
its masts are broken:
O Murshid
I take refuge in You!

The waves onrushing
crush the deck;
all that I treasured
like precious gems
has gone adrift:
O Murshid
I take refuge in You!

Anonymous

IX

Close to my house
there is a city of crystal.
There lives
my mysterious neighbor.
Never have I seen His face
for even a single moment
—His radiant face!

If my neighbor
had touched me only once
my death anguish
would have vanished . . .
But I, poor Lalan, and He,
though we live under the same sky
are separated by an immense void.
Millions of leagues,
alas, under the same sky,
separate us . . .

Lalan Fakir

X

O my heart
before whom will you prostrate yourself
to whom will you say "my guru"?

He is there beside you
He is there all around you
He lives in every thing . . .

The guru is the rice in your bowl
the guru is your soul's passion.

When your heart weeps
the guru is its tears . . .

Anonymous

. . . beneath the waters
little by little the boat is sinking
but take the risk
the last . . .
O boatman, drunk with joy
good fellow on your leprous boat!

Cling to the mast
sail with high prow
Courage! have no fear . . .

Wretched broken boat
cradle of the waves
the greedy spray caresses you
go! the eternal spell
in the bewitchment of Time!

Look, there, before you . . .
. . . the way out!

Sudharam Bâül

XII

In the Ocean of love
where every form weds Beauty—
I saw in a flash
Him who lives hidden in my heart . . .
a stream of burning
molten gold . . .
What joy! What desire!
I ran to meet Him
to seize Him in my arms.

Alas! I found nothing . . .

In vain, now, I search
I have scoured the thickets
Where are You?
I am anxious
I wander like a madman
Where are You?
A fire consumes me
In the depths of myself
which devours me
which will never be extinguished . . .

Anonymous

XIII

If in my cage
  the mysterious bird
which comes whence . . . I know not
going whither . . . I know not
  by chance would enter
  quickly I would capture it!
I wish so much
  that I could fasten
  to one of its feet
the golden chain
  of my heart . . .

Anonymous

XIV

The one who has dived into divine love
   my heart quickly recognizes
   when he visits me!
A veil of tears shines in his eyes
the shadow of a smile lights his face
   —depth of warm tenderness
   —ecstasy of infinite love
a light is kindled in the lotus of his heart
Ah! the tide of his desires is drunk up by the sand dunes
   but overcoming all the barriers
   the river of his love has flooded everything . . .

Anonymous

XV

The road towards You is blocked
by so many temples and mosques!
I indeed hear Your call clearly
O my Beloved
but I cannot move forward
gurus and murshids,
bristling, guard the passage . . .

What a dream—
to plunge into Your current
coolness of my blood
but flames arise
to devour the world.
Where is Your peace, O my Master?
Your message of unity
is covered with ashes . . .

Heavy the chains
    that close Your door
Puranas, Koran, rosaries
robes the color of fire
sow on the dusty roads
the hard seeds of pride . . .
Madan moans in pain . . .

Madan Fakir

XVI

May blessing be!
  I am an empty vessel!

When You swim in the pond
I lean against Your breast
my head turns upon Your heart
my Beloved!

Those who are full vessels
You place upon the bank
You carry them into Your house
useful for water . . .

But I, I swim with You
I breathe to the rhythm of Your joy
Your arms of love embrace me
hold me close against You.

Drunken I give myself up
to the waves of the stream
to the waves of Your love
My Love!

Anonymous

XVII

O my Beloved
if the fire of Your love
can burn without me
let us part!
There, at once . . .
. . . I go away!

Whirlwinds of dust
  noisy bazaars
furrows of embers burning
  hard distances of roads—
broken with fatigue, I walk . . .

O King of my heart
when You thirst for love
You will know how to go after me
  and find me
That is why
I have become a wanderer
on Your road
for You
—nameless
—dust!

Anonymous

XVIII

I shall not go to Mecca nor Medina
since my Beloved
is here
in me and I in Him . . .

It would be madness to go far away
it would be madness no more to see
His face in me . . .

Neither temple nor mosque
nor puja nor bakrid,
each clod of earth
—the earth I tread
is Kashi and Mecca
each instant is the shining joy
of my Beloved . . .

Anonymous

XIX

O! stubborn one, by your cruel impatience
by your merciless insistence,
by the fire do you really wish
to force tight buds to open,
flowers to bloom
and fill the air with their perfume?

Do you not see that the great Artisan, My Lord,
at his leisure, by his grace
since the night of time
has caused the flowers to open from the bud?

Guilty is your ambition
and your wish to force life;
truly your purpose is sterile
stubborn, gnawed by impatience . . .

Do you not know that the river
invites you—
silently, calm, it flows—
Give in and let yourself float
your soul filled with His melody
O stubborn one, devoured by impatience . . .

Anonymous

XX

How my heart has melted
I know not . . .
in the ecstasy of life
in the ecstasy of death
my heart is drunk with joy . . .

O Beloved
make me not languish in vain
I no longer expect anything
  from tomorrow
  nor from yesterday
Your little bells ring day and night
O miracle! I am bewildered . . .

Where is the infinite sea?
Where is the eddying river?
If you would know
the secret tide of life that makes them one,
marry your heart with your eyes.

Then in you
the eyes of your heart
will see the game of God.

Ishân Jugi, the Weaver

XXI

Oh! no one has ever found
who He is
—a fool of God—
who wanders from door to door . . .
—a beggar of love—
going from door to door . . .

Anonymous

XXII

O my spirit, rest anchored in yourself
knock not at any door.
If you go deep into yourself
you will find what you seek.

God, the true philosopher's stone
who transmutes all desires
dwells in your heart
the most beautiful of jewels.

How many pearls and diamonds
pave round about
the antechamber of your heart's pavilion!

Anonymous

XXIII

I cannot open my heart to you
   O my friend
because my lips are sealed . . .
in life's grayness
   how can I persevere
if the Beloved
   who knows all my suffering
stays so far from me?

Him who is my heart's beloved
   I would know at a glance
   But shall I ever see Him?
He passes in dreams of light
He plunges in the deeps of joy
   skillful boatman
of the high tides of divine love.

Anonymous

XXIV

Blessed am I
if the three worlds are Your flute!
  I am the wind that plays on it
  the breath of Your lips.
What harm, truly,
  if at each note I die!
Under Your fingers my notes fall one by one
  singing of good, of bad
  pouring out pleasure and pain.
I am the song of dawn and of evening
  and of the dead of night
but if it pleases You
  I can sing also
the smiles and showers of spring.
If I am the instrument of Your song
  what else could I desire?
What harm, truly,
  if at each note I die?

Ishân Jugi, the Weaver

XXV

In my soul
I hear a voice calling me
who is He—devoured with impatience
who caresses my two hands?
who is He—with flickering eyelids,
who seeks to take me in His arms?

My heart quivers
I cannot go forward
He who calls me is there . . .
His voice moves me
His song repeats without end
"Where are you going?
Oh! come, come to Me . . ."

In order not to hear Him
I fled . . .
But I walk like a blind man
—fog
in the night I walk . . .
Then turning back
there, in my heart,
I saw Him waiting for me
there, ready to welcome me . . .

Man Mohan Bâül

XXVI

And the Bâüls came
  they danced
  they sang

And they disappeared
  in the mist . . .
and the house was left empty
  empty . . . the house . . .
  in the mist . . .

     Song murmured by Shrî Râmakrishna
     shortly before he died.

THE PENGUIN METAPHYSICAL LIBRARY

Some Other Volumes in This Series